Bible Boot Camp for Military Women

THE MILITARY WOMEN OF PLANTING ROOTS

Bible Boot Camp for Military Women

THE MILITARY WOMEN OF PLANTING ROOTS

AMERICAN BIBLE SOCIETY

Philadelphia

BIBLE BOOT CAMP FOR MILITARY WOMEN

Contributors: Claudia Duff, Salena Duffy, Kristin Goodrich, Muriel Gregory, Ginger Harrington, Melissa Hicks, Suzanne Isaac, Major (Retired) Christine Malkemes, Andrea Plotner, Jennifer Wake, Kori Yates

Edited by Davina McDonald

ABS Item 124845

Design by Caleb Komorowski, Robert Giorgio, and Shannon Smith VanderWeide

Cover image by Ryan Breeden

Set in Arno Pro and Avenir

American Bible Society
101 North Independence Mall East
Philadelphia, PA 19106

www.american.bible

Printed in the United States of America

Introduction

Welcome to Bible Boot Camp, a series of three Challenges designed to help you understand the Old Testament, the New Testament, and the Bible as a whole!

Like training drills, these Challenges can be done in any order and are intended to strengthen your understanding of God's Word.

You can tackle the drills on your own or with a small team of women. A leader's guide at the end of the book can help team leaders navigate each Challenge successfully.

— *The military women of Planting Roots*

The LORD bless you and keep you;
the LORD make his face to shine upon you and be
   gracious to you;
the LORD lift up his countenance upon you and give
   you peace. (Numbers 6:24-26)

Contents

Welcome

Military units often have "Hail & Farewell" functions to welcome new members and send off others. Consider this your "Hail" and warm welcome to God's Word, the Bible.

Have you ever wanted to read the Bible yet don't know where to start? Or started at the beginning and gotten bogged down? Need a spiritual "drill sergeant" to lead you? We can help. Written for military service women, this booklet will give you a brief introduction to the Bible. It will explain the Old and New Testaments—written before and after Christ—and help you navigate God's Word with confidence.

The Bible is orderly, instructional and inspirational. It is God's self-expression. The Bible is the source of truth, wisdom, hope and encouragement. These are things all people need but especially military women who sacrifice to ensure our freedom.

Military women are uniquely positioned to understand the sacrificial nature of Christianity. Christ gave his all to buy our spiritual freedom. We will discover these themes and more in the pages of God's Word.

Here's how this study works. Each reading takes about five minutes. It includes a Bible verse and simple explanation. It also has reflective questions to journal on your own and/or discuss with others.

For additional Bible reading, there is a Daily Bible Reading Guide on page 134. You may also sign up to receive a daily devotional to accompany the daily reading.

- A Bible, complete with Old and New Testaments
- A notebook or journal to capture your thoughts
- An eagerness to grow spiritually

Each week also includes a Bible verse to memorize. Storing God's Word in your heart is a powerful and portable means of allowing God to speak to you from the inside out.

 When you see the "Boots on the Ground" symbol, look for real-life stories of military women encountering God's love and truth.

Again, a hearty hail and welcome!

Challenge 1

Basic Training

Challenge 1
Basic Training

Basic Training (Week One Memory Verse: 2 Timothy 3:16)
1. The Bible: God's Basic Training Manual (Day 1)
2. The Bible: The Commanding Officer's Intent (Day 2)
3. The Bible: God's Rescue Plan (Day 3)
4. The Bible: The Believer's M.R.E. (Day 4)
5. The Bible: An Offensive and Defensive Weapon (Day 5)

Old Testament (Week Two Memory Verse: Genesis 17:7)
1. God Staffs His Unit – Genesis, Exodus, Numbers, Leviticus, Deuteronomy (Day 1)
2. The Unit History – Books of Joshua, Judges, Ruth, 1 & 2 Samuel, I & 2 Kings, 1 & 2 Chronicles, Ezra, Nehemiah, Esther (Day 2)
3. God Frames the Mission – Wisdom Books (Day 3)
4. God Warns His People – Major Prophets (Day 4)
5. The Battleground – Minor Prophets (Day 5)

New Testament (Week Three Memory Verse: Mark 10:45)
1. Ultimate Point Man: Jesus Christ – The Gospels (Day 1)
2. Joint Operations – Acts (Day 2)
3. SOP, Part 1: Paul's Letters to the Churches (Day 3)
4. SOP, Part 2: Other Letters (Day 4)
5. After Action Review – Revelation (Day 5)

Basic Training (Day 1)
The Bible: God's Basic Training Manual

You Are Here

Every journey begins somewhere, and this one begins where you are in your lifelong journey with God. Before you read another line, take a few minutes to think about where you are. We've prepared some questions to help us know you better and to help you think about where you are before you take your next step toward God. Visit abs.bible/mil or text @MIL to 35134 to take a short survey.

Read

> All Scripture is breathed out by God and profitable for teaching, for reproof, for correction, and for training in righteousness. (2 Timothy 3:16)

Reflect

Did you know the Bible is the best-selling book of all time? The Bible is field-tested!

The military seems to have an acronym for just about everything. An acronym for creating training manuals is A.D.D.I.E.: "Audience, Design, Development, Implementation and Evaluation." Here's how the Bible is like a basic training manual:

- *Audience* – The Bible speaks to all people of the world, throughout all time. God used 40 different authors, over 1,500 years, to capture loving and life-giving words.

- *Design* – God is the ultimate designer. The Bible details God's instructions for wise living. Divided in two main sections, the Old Testament is the prequel to the New Testament.

- *Development* – The person following God's Word will develop and mature.

- *Implementation* – The Bible is the how-to guide for life, both in principle and practice. Its books-within-a-book communicate history, law, letters, instruction, prophecy, poetry, and song. God gives us all we need for life and godliness (2 Peter 1:3).

- *Evaluation* – The Bible has clear end-goals: to know and love God, and then to transform us into God's likeness.

Are you looking for wisdom about how to be healthy and whole? Do you want to find true purpose and lasting peace? The best place to start—and finish—is the Bible!

Respond

- *Journal:* On a 1-10 scale, I would number my familiarity with the Bible as a ...

- *Journal:* Questions I have about God and the Bible are...

- *Discuss:* If the Bible is God's self-expression, then...

Dear God, please make me an honest student of the Bible, open to truth. Amen (means so-be-it).

Weekly Memory Verse
All Scripture is breathed out by God and profitable for teaching, for reproof, for correction, and for training in righteousness. (2 Timothy 3:16)

Basic Training (Day 2)
The Bible: The Commanding Officer's Intent

Read

> Hear, O Israel: The LORD our God, the LORD is one. You shall love the LORD your God with all your heart and with all your soul and with all your might. And these words that I command you today shall be on your heart. You shall teach them diligently to your children, and shall talk of them when you sit in your house, and when you walk by the way, and when you lie down, and when you rise. You shall bind them as a sign on your hand, and they be as frontlets between your eyes. You shall write them on the doorposts of your house and on your gates. (Deuteronomy 6:4-9)

Reflect

Do you ever wonder about the purpose of life or, more specifically, *your* purpose in life? The "Commanding Officer's Intent" is a document describing the purpose and goals of a military organization. Each person's activity has purpose within the unit.

The Bible is like the "C.O.'s Intent." The Bible reveals the origins and meaning of life. Since God created us, he knows how we function best—that is, in right relationship with him and others. You're designed for right relationship, for community. God made you for good and glorious purposes. God gives his written Word to guide and to gift you beyond your wildest expectations —now and forever.

Knowing our goal is right relationship with God and others helps shape our activity.

When Kristin recognized faith set her apart from her military classmates, she not only listened to God by reading God's Word, but listened to others as a means of caring.

On Point: The Bible communicates our life purpose.

Respond

- *Journal*: My purpose in life up to this point has been…

- *Journal*: Being in right relationship with God and others might mean…

- *Discuss*: From Deuteronomy 6:4-9, I see God's purposes include…

God, please make the Bible and your purposes clear to me. Amen.

Weekly Memory Verse

All Scripture is breathed out by God and profitable for teaching, for reproof, for correction, and for training in righteousness. (2 Timothy 3:16)

Basic Training (Day 3)
The Bible: God's Rescue Plan

Read

> My soul longs for your salvation;
> > I hope in your word.
> My eyes long for your promise;
> > I ask, 'When will you comfort me?'
> (Psalm 119:81-82)

Reflect

Why are Disney movies so popular? They reflect truth about the struggle of good vs. evil. The Bible tells the complete, true story of good vs. evil by explaining how good wins.

The Bible shows we really do live in a broken world where bad things happen. Every day, military members put on uniforms and serve in our fallen world. But this was not God's original intent.

When you read the first book of the Bible, Genesis, you'll see God created a "heaven-on-earth" (the Garden of Eden). God gave the first people, Adam and Eve, free will and allowed them to choose between the ways of life or of death. They willfully made a bad choice and sinned by disobeying God. Sin separated us from God and left us in need of rescue.

But God has a plan to save us from this broken world where evil happens.

Imagine a water rescue, where the rescuer comes under the drowning person and moves them to the surface. God's rescue plan is fulfilled in his Son Jesus. Jesus died a sacrificial death, taking upon himself our sin and the death penalty. Jesus came to rescue us from darkness and death, and move us into light and to life in its fullness. But we must accept God's rescue, and not flail against him.

The battle is real, and the Bible tells us Jesus wins. John 3:16 says, *"For God so loved the world, that he gave his only Son, that whoever believes in him should not perish but have eternal life."* The Bible is the source of all we need to know about God's triumph over evil.

On Point: The Bible communicates God's plan to rescue us from spiritual death.

Respond

- *Journal*: I experienced a personal struggle of good vs. evil when…
- *Journal*: I need a rescue plan in these areas of my life…
- *Discuss*: Psalm 119:81-82 tells me this about God's character:

God, please help me understand sin and salvation as described in Your Word. Amen.

Weekly Memory Verse

All Scripture is breathed out by God and profitable for teaching, for reproof, for correction, and for training in righteousness. (2 Timothy 3:16)

Basic Training (Day 4)

The Bible: The Believer's M.R.E.

> Give us this day our daily bread, and forgive us our debts,
> as we also have forgiven our debtors. (Matthew 6:11-12)

Every military member knows what a M.R.E. is—a Meal, Ready-to-Eat. M.R.E.s are complete, pre-cooked, portable meals. The Bible is like the believer's M.R.E.—ideal for daily consumption. "The LORD's Prayer," is an example. It's a prayer model that Jesus introduced to his disciples in Matthew 6:

> Pray then like this:
> "Our Father in heaven,
> hallowed be your name
> Your kingdom come,
> your will be done,
>   on earth as it is in heaven.
> Give us this day our daily bread,
> and forgive us our debts,
>   as we also have forgiven our debtors.
> And lead us not into temptation,
>   but deliver us from evil." (Matthew 6:9-13)

Whether one verse or many, feeding on the Bible will keep you satisfied and strong!

Jenny, a busy military wife, doesn't like to read, so Bible "study" feels hard. God's Word can be memorized and meditated on, making it portable and powerful.

On Point: The Bible feeds us spiritually, and memorization makes it portable nourishment.

Respond

- *Journal*: The Bible is like a spiritual M.R.E. in these ways...

- *Journal*: If I prayed regularly, I think I would...

- *Discuss*: Matthew 6:9-13—The LORD's Prayer— reveals these things about God

Dear God, thank you for your Word which is portable and powerful. Help me feast on it daily. Amen.

Weekly Memory Verse

All Scripture is breathed out by God and profitable for teaching, for reproof, for correction, and for training in righteousness. (2 Timothy 3:16)

Basic Training (Day 5)

The Bible: An Offensive and Defensive Weapon

> Finally, be strong in the Lord and in the strength of his might. Put on the whole armor of God, that you may be able to stand against the schemes of the devil. For we do not wrestle against flesh and blood, but against the rulers, against the authorities, against the cosmic powers over this present darkness, against the spiritual forces of evil in the heavenly places. Therefore take up the whole armor of God, that you may be able to withstand in the evil day, and having done all, to stand firm. Stand therefore, having fastened on the belt of truth, and having put on the breastplate of righteousness, and, as shoes for your feet, having put on the readiness given by the gospel of peace. In all circumstances take up the shield of faith, with which you can extinguish all the flaming darts of the evil one; and take the helmet of salvation, and the sword of the Spirit, which is the word of God, praying at all times in the Spirit, with all prayer and supplication. To that end, keep alert with all perseverance, making supplication for all the saints. (Ephesians 6:10-11)

Reflect

We live in a spiritual battlefield and have a spiritual enemy. Have you ever felt ill equipped for a mission? God prepares us with a spiritual uniform and weapons. This weaponry is unseen but real (like emotions—invisible yet powerful). Our job is to armor up daily!

- *Belt of Truth* (Ephesians 6:14) – Know the truth and live accordingly
- *Breastplate of Righteousness* (Ephesians 6:14) – Come to God daily for inner cleansing
- *Shoes of Peace* (Ephesians 6:15) – Be ready to share the Good News of peace
- *Shield of Faith* (Ephesians 6:16) – Faith in Christ shields us from Satan's arrows
- *Helmet of Salvation* (Ephesians 6:17) – Accept the free gift of salvation Christ offers
- *Sword of the Spirit* (Ephesians 6:17) – This is the Word of God, the Bible… absorb it

On Point: The Bible is a critical part of our daily spiritual armor.

Respond

- *Journal*: I experienced life as a spiritual battlefield when…
- *Journal*: Battles in my world today include…
- *Discuss*: Ephesians 6:10-18 can encourage God's people because…

Lord, please help me put on the full armor you give so I will be well prepared for daily living. Amen.

Weekly Memory Verse

All Scripture is breathed out by God and profitable for teaching, for reproof, for correction, and for training in righteousness. (2 Timothy 3:16)

Old Testament (Day 1)

God Staffs His Unit – Genesis, Exodus, Leviticus, Numbers, Deuteronomy

Read

> And I will establish my covenant between me and you and your offspring after you throughout their generations for an everlasting covenant, to be God to you and to your offspring after you. (Genesis 17:7)

Reflect

Do you ever use finger counting to remember things? Last week we talked about the Bible in general. This week we will look at the Old Testament—the time before Christ. To sum up the Old Testament, use three fingers to remember **creation**, **law**, and **covenant**.

Creation: Genesis is the first book of the Old Testament. Genesis means "beginnings" and shows God creating light, darkness, earth, sky, sea, land, and animals. God called everything he had made, "very good" (see Genesis 1:31). Adam and Eve disobeyed one of God's instructions. As a result, sin entered the world and humanity's fellowship with God suffered. **God always wants to be in relationship with us and see us walk in his ways.**

Law: The Law was God's means of re-establishing his people. But it took a while to play out. The book of Exodus ("exit") tells of God helping his people escape from slavery in Egypt. The full law is given in the books of Leviticus ("law") and Deuteronomy ("second law").

Covenant: The first five books of the Old Testament tell of God's chosen people, the Israelites who are "numbered" by census in Numbers. God counted up his people to know who to count on. So we titled this lesson, "God Staffs His Unit." One of the senior commanders is Abraham. God makes a covenant—a binding promise—with Abraham in Genesis 17:7. God promises Abraham a permanent relationship. This special promise continues today. Jesus, whom we learn about in the New Testament, serves as God's guarantee—kind of like God's signature guaranteeing payment of his promises (see 2 Corinthians 1:20). Deep but powerful stuff!

On Point: God always wants to be in relationship with us and see us walk in his ways.

- *Journal*: The first five books of the Old Testament are...
- *Journal*: When I think about walking in the ways of God...
- *Discuss*: How can a relationship with God address loneliness?

God, thank you for the Bible—telling of your people, your promises and your plans. Amen.

Weekly Memory Verse

And I will establish my covenant between me and you and your offspring after you throughout their generations for an everlasting covenant, to be God to you and to your offspring after you. (Genesis 17:7)

Old Testament (Day 2):

The Unit History – Joshua, Judges, Ruth, 1 & 2 Samuel, I & 2 Kings, 1 & 2 Chronicles, Ezra, Nehemiah, Esther

Read

> …If my people, who are called by my name, will humble themselves and pray and seek my face and turn from their wicked ways, then will I hear from heaven and will forgive their sin and will heal their land. (2 Chronicles 7:14)

Reflect

Ever thought of history as dry, only to find a personal connection, such as in your unit's history? Yesterday we learned three key words: **creation**, **law**, and **covenant**. Today we learn more about God's care of the Israelites in what are known as "historical books." The Old Testament (OT) books of Joshua, Judges, Ruth, 1 & 2 Samuel, I & 2 Kings, 1 & 2 Chronicles, Ezra, Nehemiah, Esther relate some "unit history" that will draw you in. **The OT historical books show that God's purposes and promises are for the good of his people**. He is a loving shepherd.

As Joshua opens, God is preparing to take his people into the Promised Land—modern day Israel. In Judges, God appoints a series of leaders to provide direction and redirection. Ruth is a love story showing us God's personal care. The books of 1 & 2 Samuel and 1 & 2 Kings show the Israelites begging God for kings to rule over them, yet many leaders prove wicked. King David—a man after God's own heart—is a central figure in the Old Testament known for his readiness to repent of his wrongdoing. 1 & 2 Chronicles are temple records—seemingly uninteresting but full of **covenant** insights. Ezra, Nehemiah and Esther show Israel's return from captivity.

On Point: The OT historical books show us God's faithfulness in action.

Respond

- *Journal*: The 12 Old Testament historical books are…
- *Journal*: Bible history can teach me lessons about God in these ways…
- *Discuss*: How are the OT historical books like a military unit's history?

God, thank you for revealing your character and faithfulness in Old Testament history. Amen.

Weekly Memory Verse

And I will establish my covenant between me and you and your offspring after you throughout their generations for an everlasting covenant, to be God to you and to your offspring after you. (Genesis 17:7)

Old Testament (Day 3)
God Frames the Mission – Wisdom Books

Read

> The LORD is my shepherd; I shall not want.
> (Psalm 23:1)

Reflect

Military training is not a simple or instantaneous process. The purpose is to establish and strengthen the capabilities of military personnel while making sure they have the right attitude. Likewise, the life of faith involves all your heart, all your soul, and all your might (Deuteronomy 6:5). **The wisdom books address spiritual attitude and spiritual readiness**. In other words, they frame the mission of following God and walking in his ways.

The five wisdom (or poetry) books are Job, Psalms, Proverbs, Ecclesiastes and Song of Solomon. These books establish and strengthen God's people through praise, instruction, reflection, thanksgiving and song. You can be trained to carry a godly spiritual attitude. In Psalms and Proverbs, "establish" is mentioned forty-six times, and "strength" or "strengthen" shows up ninety-five times in the wisdom books! Hebrew poetry uses repetition of ideas more than rhyme. This helps the ideas sink in.

Other themes in the wisdom books include:

- *Job*: Suffering and God's sovereignty
- *Psalms*: Worship
- *Proverbs*: Wisdom
- *Ecclesiastes*: Meaninglessness
- *Song of Solomon*: Love

Andrea's dad, Steve, a crusty Vietnam vet, said almost every deployed service member in that era knew Psalm 23 and Psalm 91 by heart. Many years and trials later, God used those tucked-away truths to bring Steve to saving faith and daily trust in the Lord Jesus Christ.

On Point: God wants to establish and strengthen us, and be our Good Shepherd.

Respond

- *Journal*: The five wisdom books in the Old Testament are...

- *Journal*: I need to be established and strengthened by God because...

- *Discuss*: Framing the mission—my view of things—matters because...

Dear God, please give me a hunger to learn more about you through your Word, the Bible. Amen.

Weekly Memory Verse

And I will establish my covenant between me and you and your offspring after you throughout their generations for an everlasting covenant, to be God to you and to your offspring after you. (Genesis 17:7)

Old Testament (Day 4)

God Warns His People – Major Prophets:
Isaiah, Jeremiah, Lamentations, Ezekiel, Daniel

Read

> And I will give you a new heart, and a new spirit I will put
> within you. And I will remove the heart of stone from
> your flesh and give you a heart of flesh. (Ezekiel 36:26)

Reflect

There were three main types of "officers" in the Old Testament
—prophet, priest, and king. Jesus later served in all three offices.
Today we look at the prophets, specifically the Major Prophets.

Old Testament prophets were God's mouthpieces. **When you
know someone needs a warning or course correction, you
do all you can to help them, right?** Prophets served both
practical and spiritual roles.

"Major Prophets" and "Minor Prophets" do not refer to ranks
but to the length of the prophetic books. The Major Prophet
books are longer than the Minor Prophet books. Here's a
breakdown of the five Major Prophet books:

- *Isaiah*: Warned of enemy captivity; many of the
  prophet's words were later fulfilled in Jesus.

- *Jeremiah*: God cares for individuals as well as
  nations; ignoring God has consequences.

- *Lamentations*: Five poems mourning Jerusalem's
  fall; a call to return to God. (This book is
  traditionally ascribed to the prophet Jeremiah.)

- *Ezekiel*: God appeals to his people to turn away

from evil, wicked and rebellious ways.

- *Daniel*: Here we meet Daniel—one of God's faithful men—a civil servant under foreign rule.

We should expect to encounter God when we read the Bible. God's lovingkindness and his righteous ways are communicated throughout its pages and in God we find our strength.

On Point: The Major Prophet books tell us a lot about God's kindness and what pleases God.

Respond

- *Journal*: List the five Major Prophet books, and perhaps a brief description.
- *Journal*: I am/am not eager to encounter God through Bible reading because…
- *Discuss*: How can a warning be a form of kindness?

God, thank you for examples like Daniel. Please help me be attentive to your warnings. Amen.

WEEKLY MEMORY VERSE

And I will establish my covenant between me and you and your offspring after you throughout their generations for an everlasting covenant, to be God to you and to your offspring after you. (Genesis 17:7)

Old Testament (Day 5)

God's Battleground – Minor Prophets: Hosea, Joel, Amos, Obadiah, Jonah, Micah, Nahum, Habakkuk, Zephaniah, Haggai, Zechariah, and Malachi

Read

> The LORD your God is in your midst,
>   a mighty one who will save;
> he will rejoice over you with gladness;
>   he will quiet you by his love;
> he will exult over you with loud singing.
> (Zephaniah 3:17)

Reflect

This week we cover the twelve "Minor Prophet" books. Remember they're only "minor" because they're shorter. Obadiah has just 21 verses! We call this section of the Bible "God's Battleground" because each book deals with a specific sin problem. In fact, **prophetic books each tend to follow a similar pattern**—1. Warning 2. Specific sin 3. Coming judgement 4. Call to repentance and 5. Promise of future rescue. Key themes will help you remember individual books:

- *Hosea*: God is stubbornly loyal.

- *Joel*: God controls history.

- *Nahum*: God avenges injustice.

- *Habakkuk*: God is good despite evil.

- *Amos*: God is judge.
- *Obadiah*: God punishes evil.
- *Jonah*: You can't outrun God.
- *Micah*: Who is like God?
- *Zephaniah*: God restores.
- *Haggai*: God's promises give hope.
- *Zechariah*: God remembers.
- *Malachi*: God calls to repentance.

If you are facing battles in your own life—internal or external—the Minor Prophets can be brief messages of encouragement. Zephaniah 3:17 reminds us that our loving God is mighty to save!

On Point: The Minor Prophets show the lengths to which God goes to save people from sin.

Respond

- *Journal*: The twelve Minor Prophets are…
- *Journal*: Though short books, the Minor Prophets are relevant because…
- *Discuss*: Why is sin so rampant when God is so clearly against it?

Dear God, please show me any sin in my life I need to repent of, and your means of escape. Amen.

Weekly Memory Verse

And I will establish my covenant between me and you and your offspring after you throughout their generations for an everlasting covenant, to be God to you and to your offspring after you. (Genesis 17:7)

New Testament (Day 1)

Ultimate Point Man: Jesus Christ –
The Gospels: Matthew, Mark, Luke, John

Read

> For even the Son of Man came not to be served but to serve, and to give his life as a ransom for many. (Mark 10:45)

Reflect

Service. It's a concept we understand. Jesus came to serve. We learn about Jesus in the Gospels.

This week we summarize the New Testament. The Bible is divided in two main sections—before and after Jesus Christ. The first four books of the New Testament are called Gospels—meaning good news—and give us snapshots of the life of Christ. These four books are Matthew, Mark, Luke and John. Many people like to start with John. Our key verse, Mark 10:45, is just one snapshot of Christ's character—servanthood.

Who is Jesus? In the Gospels, we discover Jesus Christ is the sinless Son of God—the exact representation of the Father—and our ultimate point man. **Jesus is God's promised rescue plan**. Jesus gave his all to secure our freedom from sin and to give life everlasting for all who believe. Imagine God allowing himself to be subjected to such pain and heartache! But God did. God had power to stop the evil at any time. But our need was great: because of the destructive nature of sin, we had no hope. Jesus submitted to this suffering to rescue humanity from sin once and for all.

Salena, a single mom, was heartbroken about being separated from her young son during deployment. As a result, she had trouble functioning well. At one low point, she turned to the Gospels where she encountered Christ. This became a turning point in her heart, her life, her faith, her family and her career.

On Point: Jesus is God's promised rescue plan and the Gospels tell Jesus's story.

Respond

- *Journal*: The four books describing the life and ministry of Jesus are…

- *Journal*: Why should I follow Jesus as Lord of my life?

- *Discuss*: How is Jesus God's "rescue plan"?

Dear God, thank you for sending your sinless Son Jesus to save us. Help me grow in faith! Amen.

Weekly Memory Verse

For even the Son of Man came not to be served but to serve, and to give his life as a ransom for many. (Mark 10:45)

New Testament (Day 2)

Joint Operations – Acts

Read

> But you will receive power when the Holy Spirit
> has come upon you, and you will be my witnesses in
> Jerusalem and in all Judea and Samaria, and to the end
> of the earth. (Acts 1:8)

Reflect

The Book of Acts describes the "Joint Operations" of the early
Christian church. The operations start where the Gospels leave
off. If you have time, read Luke and Acts together as they are
both written by Dr. Luke. Acts begins as Christ ascends into
heaven. God sends the Holy Spirit—the Helper—to empower
Christ-followers throughout the world. Acts 1:8 commissions
believers to be witnesses of Christ at home and abroad.

The early believers included Jews and non-Jews called Gentiles.
They devoted themselves to teaching, fellowship, praise, prayer,
caring for the poor, and gathering in the temple and in homes
(Acts 2). Having both Jewish and Gentile members, the early
church struggled at times with integrating cultural and language
differences. Daily operations were challenging.

Peter and Paul led the operations in Acts. Peter led the
Christians headquartered in Jerusalem while Paul's teams were
deployed across the Roman empire. These operations were
empowered by the Holy Spirit, who is mentioned over fifty
times in the book of Acts.

**Acts is a must-read to understand both Christian history
and the work of the Holy Spirit!**

Being told when and where to go brings a certain comfort in military assignments. When retirement time came, Chrissy didn't know where to settle. Then she read Acts 17:26-27 which says God marks out our allotted periods and boundaries. Whatever the location or duration of her next move, job or duty station, God will be with her!

On Point: Acts describes the "Joint Operations" of the early Christian church.

Respond

- *Journal*: In my own words, Acts 1:8 says…
- *Journal*: Things I am devoted to besides God are…
- *Discuss*: Can you describe the difference between the faith presented in the Old Testament and New Testament?

God, thank you for the church! Please help me truly understand its development in Acts. Amen.

Weekly Memory Verse

For even the Son of Man came not to be served but to serve, and to give his life as a ransom for many. (Mark 10:45)

New Testament (Day 3)

SOP, Part I: Letters to the Churches –
Romans, 1 & 2 Corinthians, Galatians,
Ephesians, Philippians, Colossians,
1 & 2 Thessalonians, 1 & 2 Timothy,
Titus, Philemon

Read

> I have been crucified with Christ. It is no longer I who live, but Christ who lives in me. And the life I now live in the flesh I live by faith in the Son of God, who loved me and gave himself for me. (Galatians 2:20)

Reflect

People often identify themselves according to their occupation. "I am a Sailor," or "I work for the Navy." On a much bigger scale, seeing myself as a Christ-follower gives me a new identity. Paul, the author of Galatians, describes his new identity in Christ. He has died to himself, being "crucified with Christ," and is alive with Christ. Paul is the author of thirteen letters in the New Testament. We call these—get ready for it—Paul's Letters. Paul's letters are like the Standard Operating Procedures of the Christian life—the why and how.

Who was Paul? Think of the most passionate, talented, obnoxious yet likable person you know. That might give you a fair picture of Paul. A devout Jew, he was a deadly enemy of Christians before he had a supernatural encounter with Christ (Acts 9). After his conversion, Paul was all in. Even so, Paul took three or so years to marinate on faith before launching out on his missionary journeys. Good thing, too. He quickly faced religious persecution. Many of his letters are written from prison, yet his deep confidence in Christ and reliance upon the Holy Spirit sustained him. **Paul's life was hidden in Christ, giving him a new identity, boldness and courage**.

Paul's Roman citizenship allowed him to travel the known world and tell others about Jesus. His letters served as a follow-up to the many communities he visited. He discusses how to handle personal difficulties, false teachings, and persecution. Comparing Paul's activities to a military operator, we might call him a mix between a scout, a general, and Military Intelligence.

On Point: Paul's letters provide a foundation for Christian belief and instructions for life.

Respond

- *Journal*: Paul's thirteen letters are…
- *Journal*: The identity I most cling to is…
- *Discuss*: If someone has truly died to self and lives for Christ, then…

God, please help me understand what it really means to find my identity in you. Amen.

Weekly Memory Verse

For even the Son of Man came not to be served but to serve, and to give his life as a ransom for many. (Mark 10:45)

New Testament (Day 4)

SOP, Part 2: Other Letters – James, Hebrews, 1 & 2 Peter, 1, 2, & 3 John, and Jude

Read

> Count it all joy, my brothers, when you meet trials of various kinds, for you know that the testing of your faith produces steadfastness. And let steadfastness have its full effect, that you may be perfect and complete, lacking in nothing. If any of you lacks wisdom, let him ask God, who gives generously to all without reproach, and it will be given him. But let him ask in faith, with no doubting, for the one who doubts is like a wave of the sea that is driven and tossed by the wind. (James 1:2-6)

Reflect

In 2015, Americans watched over 15 million hours of "how to" videos on YouTube. I view this as a thirst for wisdom and instruction. Uniformed women are no exception. As a very small segment of the population, you have unique challenges demanding thoughtfulness and faith.

Yesterday we talked about Paul's Letters, named for their audiences. Today we look at the other New Testament letters, called the Other Letters (not joking). These books are Hebrews, James, 1 & 2 Peter, 1, 2 & 3 John, and Jude. Except for Hebrews, these are named for their authors, not their audiences. **These Other Letters are super practical and helpful SOPs, answering the "what should this look like and why?" of everyday faith**. Three focus areas:

- How to love God

- How to love others

- How to guard against false teaching

Also in focus is James 1:2-6, which tells us what to do when we need God's wisdom. Need wisdom? Ask God who gives generously without frowning disapproval. How to ask? Ask with single-minded faith, believing that God can and will provide. In other words, don't make God Plan B or C or D. Why ask? So that God may perfect you, giving you joy even in trials.

On Point: New Testament letters are like "Standard Operating Procedures" for the Christian.

Respond

- *Journal*: The eight "Other Letters" in the New Testament are…

- *Journal*: An area of military life that needs God's wisdom is…

- *Discuss*: What makes people seek wisdom from the Internet rather than from God?

God, thank you for the New Testament letters which equip me for life and godliness. Amen.

Weekly Memory Verse

For even the Son of Man came not to be served but to serve, and to give his life as a ransom for many. (Mark 10:45)

New Testament (Day 5)

After Action Review – Revelation

> The revelation of Jesus Christ, which God gave him to show to his servants the things that must soon take place. He made it known by sending his angel to his servant John. (Revelation 1:1)

Reflect

Mark Twain's quote "Truth is stranger than fiction" is a very fitting description of the Book of Revelation! A few fun facts about the final book of the Bible:

- Revelation, though a letter, is the only book of prophecy in the New Testament
- Revelation acts as a bookend to Genesis, the first book in the Old Testament
- **Revelation reminds us, again and again, Jesus wins**!

The author of Revelation is John, who writes as a political prisoner under house arrest. He's imprisoned for sharing his faith, and writes to "seven churches" at the Lord's prompting (Revelation 1:9-11). The seven churches are in modern-day Turkey.

Written both to warn and encourage the seven churches—and us by extension—Revelation is primarily a book of prophecy. Revelation is like a military After Action Review (AAR) and describes the end of human events followed by a victorious eternity for Christ's own people. Though fearsome and symbolic, Revelation gives God-fearers cause for great hope! Revelation is the only book of the Bible that promises a blessing to those who read it aloud, and to those who hear and obey (Revelation 1:3). That's one of many great reasons to find a community of faith!

 Unit morale was incredibly low during my basic training. Some women recycled; some went AWOL; others just couldn't get along. Though I'd first been mocked for reading my Bible, I was asked to read it aloud one night. The entire atmosphere changed from that point on.

On Point: The only New Testament book of prophecy, Revelation reminds us Jesus wins.

Respond

- *Journal*: Revelation is a book of prophecy. This means...

- *Journal*: Revelation says eternal life is real. This means...

- *Discuss*: How do thoughts of eternal life impact military life?

Lord, please help me keep in mind there is a spiritual battle raging, yet Jesus wins. Amen.

Weekly Memory Verse

For even the Son of Man came not to be served but to serve, and to give his life as a ransom for many. (Mark 10:45)

BIBLE BOOT CAMP FOR MILITARY WOMEN

Congratulations

You have completed Challenge 1! Psalm 119:130 says, "The unfolding of your words gives light." And we hope that's been your experience whether you tackled this Challenge as an individual or part of a small group.

Remember this is a three-part training program to familiarize you with the Bible! Dig out that determination and get ready for the next Challenge! You can do it!

Challenge 2

Old Testament

Challenge 2

Old Testament

History (Week One Memory Verse: 1 Samuel 12:24)

1. God is Creator – Genesis (Day 1)
2. God Rescues – Exodus (Day 2)
3. God Instructs – Leviticus, Numbers, and Deuteronomy (Day 3)
4. God Gives Second Chances – Joshua, Judges, Ruth (Day 4)
5. God Writes Our Biography – 1 & 2 Samuel, 1 & 2 Kings, 1 & 2 Chronicles, Ezra, Nehemiah, Esther (Day 5)

Literature (Week Two Memory Verse: Proverbs 1:7)

1. God Sees Our Struggles – Job (Day 1)
2. God is Worthy of Praise – Psalms (Day 2)
3. God Gives Wisdom – Proverbs (Day 3)
4. God Gives Life Meaning – Ecclesiastes (Day 4)
5. God is Intimate – Song of Solomon (Day 5)

Relationships (Week Three Memory Verse: Zephaniah 3:17)

1. God Warns – Isaiah, Jeremiah, Lamentations, Ezekiel (Day 1)
2. God Is in the Danger Zone – Daniel (Day 2)
3. God Directs – Hosea, Joel, Amos, Obadiah (Day 3)
4. God Course Corrects – Jonah, Micah, Nahum, Habakkuk (Day 4)
5. God Rebuilds – Zephaniah, Haggai, Zechariah, Malachi (Day 5)

Introduction

Do you recall when you joined the military? For me, it was new, challenging, and even a little scary because I was entering a whole new world. It's much the same when you join forces with God, our heavenly Commander-in-Chief. The learning curve can be steep, but we hope to guide you as you navigate it. You might even be thinking: *Are there any Christian drill sergeants out there and when do I start boot camp?*

God knew we would need guidance and instruction and gave us a manual—the Bible. It's more than a training manual, it's our manual for life. It's more than a "know how" book; it opens our eyes to God's character, thoughts and plans for us.

This Challenge is an introduction to the Old Testament, the first part of the Christian Bible.

The Old Testament (OT) is a collection of 39 books full of God-inspired history, poetry and song. A key word of the Old Testament is "Israelites." We know them today as the Jewish people. The Old Testament tells their story from the beginning. It shows how God used this people group to unfold his plan of salvation.

God's salvation is culminated in Jesus Christ, the subject of the New Testament (NT).

Suggested Supplies

- A Bible, complete with Old and New Testaments
- A notebook or journal to capture your thoughts
- An eagerness to grow spiritually

Each week also includes a Bible verse to memorize. Storing God's Word in your heart is a powerful and portable means of allowing God to speak to you from the inside out.

 When you see the "Boots on the Ground" symbol, look for real-life stories of military women encountering God's love and truth.

History (Day 1)

God Creates – Genesis

You Are Here

If this Challenge is your starting point in our Bible study, please take a few minutes to think about where you are on your lifelong journey with God. We've prepared some questions to help us know you better and to help you think about where you are before you take your next step toward God. Visit abs.bible/mil or text @MIL to 35134 to take a short survey.

Read

> God created man in his own image, in the image of God he created him; male and female he created them. (Genesis 1:27)

Reflect

Think about the beginning of your story. Does your military story begin when you were sworn in? What do these stories reveal? Every story needs a beginning. God's story begins in Genesis, which means "beginnings" or "origins." **The first book of the Bible tells of the beginning of the world, of human history, of family, and of salvation.**

Genesis contains seven stories. The first is the story of creation. How did this universe come about? How did we get here? The story of Adam and Eve is about the birth of good and evil, and how we struggle between the two.

The second is the story of Adam and the extra duties he was assigned after being kicked out of the garden of Eden for disobeying God.

Third we meet Noah. He and his family were spared from the great flood because he obeyed God and built an ark. Then, we meet Abraham who was asked by God to PCS to a "To Be Determined" location. Through hard periods of testing, Abraham remained faithful to God.

Isaac's story is next. He is the spared son of Abraham. Sixth, we meet Jacob, injured after a supernatural encounter, after which he is given a new name, Israel. This marks the beginning of the story of the Hebrew nation. Last, but not least, comes the story of Joseph who, through a whirlwind of events, becomes the second in command in Egypt.

Can you see any connection between these stories and your military life?

On Point: Genesis sets the stage for God's purpose in creation.

Respond

- *Journal*: From Genesis 1:27 I understand that…
- *Journal*: Seeing God as Creator affects my military story in these ways…
- *Discuss*: Believing that God is Creator means…

God, teach me to see you as Creator and show me how my military life is part of your story. Amen.

Weekly Memory Verse

Only fear the LORD and serve him faithfully with all your heart. For consider what great things he has done for you. (1 Samuel 12:24)

History (Day 2)
God Rescues – Exodus

> And Moses said to the people, "Fear not! Stand firm, and see the salvation of the LORD, which he will work for you today. For the Egyptians whom you see today, you shall never see again. The LORD will fight for you, and you have only to be silent." (Exodus 14:13-14)

Reflect

The word "exodus" means *exit*. The book of Exodus tells of God's good exit strategy for his people, the Hebrews. God always has an exit strategy or rescue plan for his people (see 1 Corinthians 10:13).

The Hebrews had been living in Egypt since the time of Joseph. They grew in numbers and quickly became an inside threat to the Egyptians. They were enslaved and used as forced labor. The oppression was so intolerable that they cried to God for a way out. Their rescue was coordinated by Moses, a Hebrew raised in Pharaoh's Egyptian court. After intense negotiations, Pharaoh let them go, only to change his mind and chase after them.

The Hebrews quickly found themselves at an impasse. They were trapped on one side by the Red Sea and on the other side as the Egyptians armed units approached. **But God**... God had made a promise to Abraham and Isaac and Jacob, and God was about to make good on his promises. He was the one performing the ultimate rescue with one of the most dramatic miracles in the Bible. God split the Red Sea so the Hebrews could walk through it to safety, and then ended the Egyptian enemy pursuit. Exit strategy indeed!

On Point: Throughout Exodus, God rescues his people through personal and strategic care.

- *Journal*: Exodus describes God's exit strategy for...

- *Journal*: Is there an area of my life needing God's rescue?

- *Discuss*: What does Exodus 14:13-14 reveal about God's character?

God, help me remember that you protect and rescue your people. Amen.

Only fear the LORD and serve him faithfully with all your heart. For consider what great things he has done for you. (1 Samuel 12:24)

History (Day 3)

God Instructs – Leviticus, Numbers, and Deuteronomy

> You shall love the LORD your God with all your heart and with all your soul and with all your might. And these words that I command you today shall be on your heart. (Deuteronomy 6:5-6)

Military law addresses a specific population. God's Law in the Old Testament did the same. Can you imagine a law office with law books lining the walls? That's kind of the role the first five books of the Bible (*Genesis, Exodus, Leviticus, Numbers, Deuteronomy*) play. These five books are also known as the *Pentateuch* (Five Books) or *The Torah* (Law). **Brainiac alert—these are big ideas!**

For years, scholars have studied these five books and find **they teach who God is, his love for his people, and his concern for their day-to-day welfare**. In these five books, God gives the Law to set his people apart from other nations. The Ten Commandments are concise instructions of God's protective law for his people. Leviticus (Law) and Deuteronomy (Second Law) provide detailed instructions of the entire Law.

The Old Testament could also be called the Old Covenant. A covenant is a solemn, binding promise or contract. God made a covenant with Abraham and his descendants to be their God (Genesis 17:7). In the *New* Testament, or *New* Covenant, Christ fulfills God's Law and promises. The entire book of Hebrews explains this, but Hebrews 9:15 is explicit: *For this reason Christ is the mediator of a new covenant, that those who are called may receive the promised eternal inheritance—now that he has died as a ransom to set them free from the sins committed under the first covenant* (NIV). God is a God who honors promises and contracts! Christ is his signature.

If you are a detail person (and even if you're not), consider reading the Law books and then the book of Hebrews back-to-back. Every verse and every detail in the Bible reveals some aspect of God's character and love. The detailed specifications for the Old Testament Tabernacle is one beautiful example.

On Point: God gave the Old Testament Law to reveal humanity's sinfulness and instruct his people on righteous living.

Respond

- *Journal:* The five Law Books in the Bible are…
- *Journal:* I can take comfort in God's instructions for his people because…
- *Discuss:* Compare Deuteronomy 6:5-6 and the Uniformed Code of Military Justice.

God, I pray I will see rightly and choose wisely. Amen.

Weekly Memory Verse

Only fear the LORD and serve him faithfully with all your heart. For consider what great things he has done for you. (1 Samuel 12:24)

History (Day 4)

God Gives Second Chances – Joshua, Judges, Ruth

Read

> Only be strong and very courageous, being careful to do according to all the law that Moses my servant commanded you. Do not turn from it to the right hand or to the left, that you may have good success wherever you go. [...] Have I not commanded you? Be strong and courageous. Do not be frightened, and do not be dismayed, for the LORD your God is with you wherever you go. (Joshua 1:7,9)

Reflect

God is a God of second chances. I like second chances. If I fail or mess up, I like to have the opportunity to try again. The Israelites get many second chances in Joshua, Judges, and Ruth.

Joshua is an inspiring book of military victory. In today's verses, Joshua has been commissioned by God to lead the Israelites into the Promised Land. They'd been wandering 40 years because of disobedience. Second chance! Joshua fought fear by remembering God is always near.

Judges picks up at the end of Joshua's life. No one has assumed command and the Israelites no longer follow God's commands. They repeatedly betray good order and godly discipline, so God raises up a series of judges to lead. The Israelites repeatedly cycle through second chances.

Ruth—a love story—is a welcome break from the battles, bloodshed, and backsliding in Joshua and Judges. Ruth reminds us that even when things look bleak, God has plans for good.

 Like Joshua, I learned obedience and courage as a Marine Candidate leading a platoon of OCS candidates through the woods. It took following a compass, trusting my leaders, teammates and training, plus obedience to step out. I thought we'd failed until we met our captain at the other end. She was proud of our record time. I'm glad I had the courage to step into the unknown!

On Point: God is compassionate and offers us second chances when we turn to him.

Respond

- *Journal*: Obedience to God's rules is crucial because...
- *Journal*: The story of Ruth shows me that even I...
- *Discuss*: While in uniform, I was given a second chance when ...

God, help me be strong and courageous, like Joshua. Amen.

Weekly Memory Verse

Only fear the LORD and serve him faithfully with all your heart. For consider what great things he has done for you. (1 Samuel 12:24)

History (Day 5)

God Writes Our Biography – 1 & 2 Samuel, 1 & 2 Kings, 1 & 2 Chronicles, Ezra, Nehemiah, Esther

Read

> Only fear the LORD and serve him faithfully with all your heart. For consider what great things he has done for you. (1 Samuel 12:24)

Reflect

God's people wanted a king like all their neighbors. The prophet Samuel—God's mouthpiece—warned of the consequences, which play out in the books that follow. These nine Old Testament historical books are chock-full of biographies about individuals who influence nations.

1 & 2 Samuel, 1 & 2 Kings, and 1 & 2 Chronicles are filled with adventure, rebellion, and intrigue. Some kings were mighty; some were not. The nation of Israel fell to foreign invaders.

The books of Ezra and Nehemiah were written while Israel was under occupation. Most Israelites were living far from home as refugees. These books remind us that even when we are defeated, we too can rebuild our lives and continually serve God.

Esther was a young girl who was exiled from her country and separated from her family. She was faced with a command decision: make a bold, public, risky decision or remain quiet, safe, and below the radar. **Esther reminds us that our lives, our biographies, can make a difference**. With courage and the guidance of a mentor, she risked her life and saved an entire nation.

We serve under a variety of leadership styles in the military. Think of a good leader who impacted and influenced you. Ask God to help you be that woman in the lives of others.

On Point: A life lived for God can make a dramatic difference.

-     *Journal*: What does today's verse reveal about fearing God?
-     *Journal*: One way I can act like Esther and make a difference is by…
-     *Discuss*: If God wrote my change of command biography, he would mention…

God, I pray I can clearly see your plan for my life and have the courage to follow through with it. Amen.

Only fear the LORD and serve him faithfully with all your heart. For consider what great things he has done for you. (1 Samuel 12:24)

Literature (Day 1)

God Sees Our Struggles – Job

Read

Then Job answered the LORD and said:
"I know that you can do all things,
    and that no purpose of yours can be thwarted."
(Job 42:1-2)

Reflect

Some people avoid reading the Book of Job because of the descriptions of pain and suffering. Pain and suffering are major themes. Yet, Job teaches us a crucial lesson—**God is in control even when bad things happen to good people**. This knowledge is invaluable in helping us respond to our own problems. Knowing this helps us face suffering with patience and perspective.

Life is hard whether you're a Christian or not. No one is exempt from tragedy, but as Christians we have an advantage. No, our lives are not easier. Sometimes they are even more challenging. God, whose pay grade is far above ours, is faithful, compassionate and merciful to be our battle buddy, no matter our rank.

Job was a rich and faithful man. He was definitely one of the "good people." God allowed Satan to tempt Job to doubt God's goodness and power. Bad things happened. Yet even in Job's most painful circumstances, God was steadfast. God was trustworthy. God was in control.

Job had many questions for God and requested to speak freely with God.

In the end, Job received something better than a medal: he saw God more than he saw his pain.

On Point: God is with us in our pain.

Respond

- *Journal*: Bad things happen to good military women when…
- *Journal*: Some questions I have for God are…
- *Discuss*: How can we know God is in control?

God, thank you for walking with me through the struggles of military life. Amen.

Weekly Memory Verse

The fear of the LORD is the beginning of knowledge; fools despise wisdom and instruction. (Proverbs 1:7)

Literature (Day 2)

God Is Worthy of Praise – Psalms

Read

> Great is the LORD, and greatly to be praised,
>   and his greatness is unsearchable.
> (Psalm 145:3)

Reflect

What makes a song resonate deep in our souls? Music can express what words alone often can't. The Book of Psalms, a collection of 150 poems, produce some of our best-loved songs and prayers for this very reason. They express heartfelt, gut-wrenching emotions:

-   Love for God and sorrow over sin
-   Dependence on God in desperate times
-   Thankfulness
-   Confidence in the future with God

The Psalms give us words and lyrics we can use to praise God's character. As we read these songs, we learn how to worship God with adoration and thanksgiving. The Psalms are intimate. David and other writers probably wrote the Psalms as personal poems. Authentic relationship with God is an underlying theme, reminding us that our relationship with God is not one-sided. Psalms show how to communicate in words with a holy God.

One day, her mission was to define personnel requirements for selected units in the future. As she wrote down the requirements, she began to worry: What if I was wrong? What if they don't have enough personnel to accomplish their mission, a matter of life and death? During this time, she found comfort in Psalm 16:7: "I bless the LORD who gives me counsel; in the night also my heart instructs me. She bowed her head and asked the Lord to give her counsel regarding her work, and help her not to worry."

On Point: Praising God recalibrates our hearts.

Respond

- *Journal*: Try it! A is for God's _____, B is for God's _____, C is for God's _____, etc.

- *Journal*: God's greatness is seen…

- *Discuss*: What are some ways we can praise God?

God, you are great and worthy to be praised; there is no one like you! Amen.

Weekly Memory Verse

The fear of the LORD is the beginning of knowledge; fools despise wisdom and instruction. (Proverbs 1:7)

Literature (Day 3)
God Gives Wisdom – Proverbs

Read

> For the LORD gives wisdom;
> > from his mouth come knowledge
> > and understanding.
> (Proverbs 2:6)

Reflect

In basic training, we quickly learn to do the right thing the right way every time. Everyone must make the bed with precision, fold or iron the uniform to specifications, and, let's not forget, shine those boots. When performed incorrectly, we know it right away, as does everyone else. The lazy and the incompetent negatively impact unit performance.

The Book of Proverbs is like basic training in spiritual living. Its goal is to describe and train God's people to use wisdom given by the Lord. Proverbs is written as a manual full of direct orders. Practical details, everyday situations, and valued relationships are covered. What Proverbs shows us is an all-wise God who will lead us in the way we should go. Contrary to popular opinion, God's ways are not designed to omit fun. Rather, they protect us and prepare us to experience not just the good, but the best.

Reading Proverbs is enjoyable, but I've tried to read Proverbs in one sitting and it's difficult. It's like driving without brakes. Proverbs is so powerful and instructive it requires time for pausing, thinking, and application. Time in Proverbs is time well spent!

I spent three years under a commander so tough I was tempted to go AWOL daily. I repeatedly cried to the Lord for relief. At my next assignment, I discovered I had become very capable and tenacious. In his wisdom, God had given me strength rather than relief.

On Point: God's wise ways prepare us to experience the best in life.

Respond

- *Journal*: Do I think of God's wise ways as life giving or limiting? Why?
- *Journal*: I need God's wisdom to…
- *Discuss*: Share how the book of Proverbs is like a spiritual training manual.

God, your thoughts and ways are higher than my thoughts. Help me to lean on you. Amen.

Weekly Memory Verse

The fear of the LORD is the beginning of knowledge; fools despise wisdom and instruction. (Proverbs 1:7)

Literature (Day 4)

God Gives Life Meaning – Ecclesiastes

Read

> For apart from him who can eat or who can have enjoyment? (Ecclesiastes 2:25)

Reflect

Have you ever wondered about the meaning of life? So did the writer of Ecclesiastes. Many Christians believe that the "Preacher" mentioned in the opening verse is the wise King Solomon.

If you like philosophy and thinking big thoughts, you will especially enjoy Ecclesiastes. It records the search for meaning. The theme of Ecclesiastes is the importance of fearing God in a fallen world. Though rich and powerful, the Preacher sought meaning in the many pleasures of life yet still felt empty.

Like the rest of the wisdom books, Ecclesiastes offers wisdom and knowledge to the people of God. The tragic reality of The Fall (i.e. Adam and Eve's sin) is woven throughout this book. The Preacher makes us painfully aware that all creation experiences futility and death. The "vanity of life" is mentioned at least 38 times.

Everyone and everything is affected by futility and death. Work, pleasure, survival…nothing holds value outside of relationship with God. The conclusion drawn is that those who fear the Lord are better off.

All vanity should drive us to take refuge in God whose work endures forever. Only in God is real meaning found.

Doing life without God is just life. Doing life with God is life with a capital L!

On Point: The meaning of Life (with a capital L) is found in God and God alone.

- *Journal*: How does The Fall affect you personally?
- *Journal*: Until now, I have searched for meaning in...
- *Discuss*: How does doing Life with God affect my military service?

O Lord, help me to find significance and meaning in life in you alone. Amen.

The fear of the LORD is the beginning of knowledge; fools despise wisdom and instruction. (Proverbs 1:7)

Literature (Day 5)

God is Intimate – Song of Solomon

Read

> Set me as a seal upon your heart,
>> as a seal upon your arm,
> for love is as strong as death,
>> jealousy is fierce as the grave.
> Its flashes are flashes of fire,
>> the very flame of the LORD.
> (Song of Solomon 8:6)

Reflect

The *Song of Solomon* or *Song of Songs* contains beautiful and sensuous poetry expressing romantic love between a young man (a shepherd) and a young woman (a shepherdess). Sexual activity is implied in several places. The couple's love leads to marriage, then to a life-giving physical union. This is God's way—pure, unashamed intimacy, and fruitfulness.

Song of Songs has often been interpreted by Christians as a picture of the relationship between Christ and the church.

Like other wisdom books, the Song of Songs assumes the God of Israel is the one true God, maker of heaven and earth. God's goal for love is to repair the fallen and damaged relationship with his people. Song of Songs captures God's alluring beauty and mystery.

In Ephesians 5:23, Paul compares the relationship between Christ and the church to an earthly marriage (one that is characterized by trust and loyalty). In Song of Solomon 7:10, the cherished refrain of belonging to the beloved is a picture of intimacy in marriage—a fitting image of God's relationship with his people.

 As a single Sailor, Kristin chose social activities which reinforced her desire to be sexually pure. Complex relationships gave her the opportunity to know God better since she had to spend time praying and studying the Bible. Now married, she is intimate with her Air Force husband.

On Point: God's love for us is intimate and attractive.

Respond

- *Journal*: In what ways has God shown himself to be personal in your life?
- *Journal*: On a scale of 1-10, how attractive is God's love?
- *Discuss*: Does the current culture's definition of marriage affect the picture of God's love?

God, thank you for knowing me so intimately and yet loving me unconditionally. Amen.

Weekly Memory Verse

The fear of the LORD is the beginning of knowledge; fools despise wisdom and instruction. (Proverbs 1:7)

Relationships (Day 1)

God Warns – Isaiah, Jeremiah, Lamentations, Ezekiel

Read

> I will take you from the nations and gather you from all the countries and bring you into your own land. I will sprinkle clean water on you, and you shall be clean from all your uncleannesses, and from all your idols I will cleanse you. (Ezekiel 36:24-25)

Reflect

Today we discuss four of the five Major Prophet books. A few fun facts:

1. Major Prophet books are simply longer than Minor Prophet books, not better.

2. There are five Major Prophet books but just four authors (Jeremiah wrote Lamentations)

3. Each of the four authors/prophets/messengers is a historically recognized person.

Many consider Isaiah the greatest prophet. He called the people to turn from sin and warned of God's judgement. **Return, repent and be renewed**. The first half of Isaiah is filled with warnings, but the second half is about hope.

Jeremiah is often called the "gloom and doom prophet." The people were warned, in power and truth, about what would happen if they continued to associate with the enemy. Lamentations teaches that disobedience invites ruin. But God's love is so intimate that God suffers when his people suffer. Jeremiah laments over their stubbornness.

Ezekiel preaches to deaf ears. He warns of judgment and reveals God's plan for salvation, but God's people are disloyal and suffer as a result. Yet God's tender love remains with them.

On Point: Old Testament prophecy shows that God's hard truths and warnings keep us safe.

Respond

- *Journal*: When I decide to ignore God and do things my way, I risk...
- *Journal*: In order to remain in God's safety zone...
- *Discuss*: As military Christians, we can keep each other accountable by...

God, I pray that I will listen to your warnings, stay safe, and know that you are God. Amen.

Weekly Memory Verse

The LORD your God is in your midst,
     a mighty one who will save;
he will rejoice over you with gladness;
     he will quiet you by his love;
he will exult over you with loud singing.
(Zephaniah 3:17)

Relationships (Day 2)

God IS in the Danger Zone – Daniel

Read

> He reveals deep and hidden things; he knows what is in
> the darkness, and the light dwells with him. (Daniel 2:22)

Reflect

As a female warrior, you'll be particularly wowed and inspired by
Daniel's character and courage in the danger zone. Five Reasons
Daniel Should Be Among Your Real Heroes:

1. Daniel was among the best and brightest young
    men of Israel. Think top candidates for elite
    programs. Daniel's God-given wisdom and skill
    were 10 times better than the Babylonians'. His
    three friends were in the same category.

2. Daniel won favor with foreign officials though
    enslaved and unapologetically devout.

3. Daniel found stability in God's character, not
    outward circumstances.

4. Daniel was perceptive—a student of God's Word,
    history and current events.

5. Daniel remained faithful even in the danger zone
    (lion's den).

Twenty-five centuries ago, Daniel could have given up when he
was deported to Babylon (in modern-day Iraq). He served in the
government nearly 70 years during the reigns of Nebuchadnezzar,
Belshazzar, Darius and Cyrus. Led by a madman and surrounded by
foreign gods, Daniel could have lost hope. Instead, this courageous
young man made a stand and held fast to his faith in God. Despite

circumstances, Daniel knew God was present, God had a plan, and God was sovereign. We can have the same confidence!

 Adam Curtis is a real military hero. His wife was visiting Adam during his overseas assignment when they both were detained by rogue, enemy soldiers. Despite interrogations and abuse, they remained steadfast as faithful Christians and as proud members of the military community.

On Point: Knowing that God is in control can give us courage like Daniel's.

Respond

- *Journal*: Daniel could have given up because…
- *Journal*: When times are hard, I will remember…
- *Discuss*: Daniel is an example for service members because…

God, thank you for being there even in the darkest times. Amen.

Weekly Memory Verse

The LORD your God is in your midst,
a mighty one who will save;
he will rejoice over you with gladness;
he will quiet you by his love;
he will exult over you with loud singing.
(Zephaniah 3:17)

Relationships (Day 3)

God Governs His People – Hosea, Joel, Amos, Obadiah

Read

> "Yet even now," declares the LORD, "return to me with all your heart, with fasting, with weeping, and with mourning; and rend your hearts and not your garments." Return to the LORD your God, for he is gracious and merciful, slow to anger, and abounding in steadfast love; and he relents over disaster. (Joel 2:12-13)

Reflect

The Minor Prophet books remind us of major truths such as the fact that God governs his people with truth *and* grace.

Hosea: God commanded the prophet Hosea to marry a woman who would be unfaithful and cause him anguish. In this short book, **God reveals his constant and persistent love for his people despite their wandering hearts**.

Joel: Before the Babylonian army destroyed Jerusalem, Joel served people who had taken God for granted because of peace and prosperity. Joel warned the people of imminent combat operations and urged them to turn back to God.

Amos: Justice! What does it mean? God's people sold their poor fellow Israelite brothers and sisters into slavery for profit. Will the offender get their just due? God warns that unjust, illegal, and immoral behavior will not go unpunished.

Obadiah: This one-chapter book is short, but not insignificant. Take a few moments to read through it and gain a better understanding about the way God judges those who harm his people.

On Point: The Minor Prophets show that God governs his people with truth and grace.

- *Journal*: I understand God's justice is...

- *Journal*: One way I can remain faithful to God is by...

- *Discuss*: What could happen if I fail to obey a lawful general order written by God...

God, thank you for your unfailing love and patience as you govern my life. Amen.

The LORD your God is in your midst,
    a mighty one who will save;
he will rejoice over you with gladness;
    he will quiet you by his love;
he will exult over you with loud singing.
(Zephaniah 3:17)

Relationships (Day 4)

God Course Corrects – Jonah, Micah, Nahum, Habakkuk

Read

> He has told you, O man, what is good; and what does the LORD require of you but to do justice, and to love kindness, and to walk humbly with your God? (Micah 6:8)

Reflect

Each of the Minor Prophets spoke to particular people groups yet **God's truths are universal**.

The prophet Jonah did not want to go to the Ninevites, so he boarded a ship and sailed in the opposite direction. Despite Jonah's disobedience, God re-routed him so he could pass along the message of grace and salvation. Not even the stormy sea or being swallowed by a great fish could stop God's message, or God's messenger, Jonah.

In seven short chapters, Micah paints a picture of God Almighty who hates sin but loves sinners. Micah declared judgment and yet the message of hope and restoration continued.

Nahum pronounced God's judgment. God is slow to anger and abounding in love, yet God will not let guilt go unpunished.

Habakkuk wanted answers. He was troubled by what he saw and asked God some difficult questions. *"Why is there evil in the world? Why do the wicked appear to be winning?"* God answers the difficult questions and we rejoice with Habakkuk as he gains a new understanding of God's love.

On Point: The Minor Prophets show that God gives life-giving coordinates and course corrections.

Respond

- *Journal*: Even when I stray, God…
- *Journal*: I can correct the course of my life by…
- *Discuss*: How can a leader declare judgment and hope to junior unit personnel?

God, I am thankful that you are my GPS and that you keep me on track. Amen.

Weekly Memory Verse

> The LORD your God is in your midst,
>   a mighty one who will save;
> he will rejoice over you with gladness;
>   he will quiet you by his love;
> he will exult over you with loud singing.
> (Zephaniah 3:17)

Relationships (Day 5)

God Rebuilds – Zephaniah, Haggai, Zechariah, Malachi

Read

> But for you who fear my name, the sun of righteousness shall rise with healing in its wings. You shall go out leaping like calves from the stall. (Malachi 4:2).

Reflect

Fear has many connotations. On one hand, it implies terror. On the other hand, it is a gift to keep us safe from danger. Other meanings include reverence, awe, wonder and respect. These meanings are wrapped up in being a God-fearer—one who knows both God's holiness and love. Malachi 4:2 tells us that God will vindicate and restore his people. Healing, peace, joy, and freedom are beautiful things! The Minor Prophet books include more insights on how to walk in God's healing and hopeful ways.

Prophets have the delicate task to speak God's truth, bring people out of their complacent ways, and then lead them back to safety. The people simply ignored Zephaniah. Staying comfortable is easier than breaking a bad habit. **Returning to God can be a hard—but always healing—choice**.

Haggai wrote to the people in Jerusalem urging them to complete the rebuilding of the temple. Their priorities were skewed and they had decided to focus on themselves rather than God.

Zechariah's message has the same mission statement: rebuild the temple. The rebuilding is not in vain. Hope is on the way. Of all the minor prophets, the book of Zechariah contains the most prophecies regarding Jesus.

Malachi is the last book of the Old Testament. It clearly points to Israel's unfaithfulness and the fact that guilt will be punished. Placed strategically throughout the book of Malachi are messages of hope and the possibility of forgiveness.

On Point: God's love means he will repair brokenness and rebuild with grace and truth.

Respond

- *Journal*: Being a God-fearer means…

- *Journal*: I can put God first in my life by…

- *Discuss*: What does it mean to fear God's name, as in Malachi 4:2?

God, please repair the broken places in my life. Amen.

Weekly Memory Verse

The LORD your God is in your midst,
    a mighty one who will save;
he will rejoice over you with gladness;
    he will quiet you by his love;
he will exult over you with loud singing.
(Zephaniah 3:17)

Congratulations

You have completed Challenge 2! Psalm 119:130 says, "The unfolding of your words gives light." And we hope that's been your experience whether you tackled this Challenge as an individual or part of a small group.

Remember this is a three-part training program to familiarize you with the Bible! Dig out that determination and get ready for the next Challenge! You can do it!

Challenge 3

New Testament

Challenge 3
New Testament

Jesus, Point Man (Week One Memory Verse: Matthew 1:22-23)

1. Jesus, Our Rescuer – Matthew (Day 1)
2. Jesus, Our Servant Leader – Mark (Day 2)
3. Jesus Came for All – Luke (Day 3)
4. Jesus Is God – John (Day 4)
5. Powered by the Holy Spirit – Acts (Day 5)

Letters to Churches (Week Two Memory Verse: Romans 8:1)

1. SOP of Salvation – Romans (Day 1)
2. Attention to Orders! – 1 & 2 Corinthians (Day 2)
3. Armored Up! – Galatians and Ephesians (Day 3)
4. Run the Race! – Philippians and Colossians (Day 4)
5. Firm Under Fire – 1 & 2 Thessalonians (Day 5)

Letters to Individuals and General Instructions (Week Three Memory Verse: James 3:13)

1. Mentors Matter – 1 & 2 Timothy, Titus, Philemon (Day 1)
2. Jesus is Best – Hebrews (Day 2)
3. Become Qualified – James, 1 & 2 Peter (Day 3)
4. Move Out! – 1, 2, & 3 John, Jude (Day 4)
5. Best. Ending. Ever. – Revelation (Day 5)

Introduction

Welcome to Bible Boot Camp New Testament! This three-week study guide is written for the active duty military service woman interested in learning more about Christ, Christianity, the Bible, and the New Testament, in particular.

Why study the New Testament? Christians believe it points the way to life and salvation as it tells how to know, and be known by, Jesus the Savior.

The New Testament—a collection of 27 books and letters inspired by God—is a source of life and hope. It chronicles the life and times of Jesus and the early Christian church, and it tells us how to walk by faith and not by sight, and of what is yet to come.

Wherever I am, whatever my circumstances, God sees me (and you!). The New Testament tells me God created me and loves me. God knows me intimately, down to the very number of hairs on my head (Matthew 10:30; Luke 12:7)! And God has a plan for me. It is a good plan, with my well-being in mind. Any guidance God might give is not to limit my freedom but to expand my protection and peace.

As military women, these concepts of protection and peace are not foreign. I hope you will see, as we walk through the basic setup of the New Testament, how experience with military life can help us understand the kingdom of God in special ways.

Suggested Supplies

This study is set up with one weekly lesson and five days of short devotional thoughts. Although this guide is portable and does not require extra equipment, you might find it helpful to have:

- A Bible, complete with Old and New Testaments

- A notebook or journal to capture your thoughts
- An eagerness to grow spiritually

Each week also includes a Bible verse to memorize. Storing God's Word in your heart is a powerful and portable means of allowing God to speak to you from the inside out.

 When you see the "Boots on the Ground" symbol, look for real-life stories of military women encountering God's love and truth.

I'm glad you're here! Let's ruck up and get started!

Jesus, Point Man (Day 1)

Jesus, Our Rescuer – Matthew

You Are Here

If this Challenge is your starting point in our Bible study, please take a few minutes to think about where you are on your lifelong journey with God. We've prepared some questions to help us know you better and to help you think about where you are before you take your next step toward God. Visit abs.bible/mil or text @MIL to 35134 to take a short survey.

Read

> All this took place to fulfill what the Lord had spoken by the prophet: "Behold, the virgin shall conceive and bear a son, and they shall call his name Immanuel" (which means, God with us). (Matthew 1:22-23)

Reflect

There's an acronym for clear and concise military writing: B.L.U.F.—Bottom Line Up Front. The bottom line of the Gospel of Matthew is this: Jesus is THE ONE we've been waiting for!

Matthew was written by a Jew about a Jew for a Jewish audience, saying Jesus is the one!

Matthew knew his readers were looking for a Messiah—the Jewish term for Rescuer. God had not communicated with his people for the past 400 years (since the Old Testament book of Malachi), and they were living under a harsh regime. People needed some good news, some hope. Much of the Old Testament contains promises (or prophecies) about the coming of this Messiah-Rescuer.

Matthew's main purpose was to show them (and us) that Jesus is the answer, the fulfillment of these promises. The Bible, up until this point, pointed to Jesus as the in-bound rescuer.

Through his description of Jesus's life, death, and resurrection, Matthew makes the case that Jesus is the one senior commander for whom everyone was waiting. Many in Matthew's day missed this because Jesus did not bring literal freedom from their oppressors (the Romans). Remember that some mission objectives about Jesus have yet to be executed! In the meantime, Jesus rescues us from sin and its eternal consequences. Temporary military rescue pales in comparison.

On Point: Jesus is the fulfillment of all God's promised rescue—both now and in the future!

Respond

- *Journal*: By Jesus fulfilling these promises, I understand that…

- *Journal*: I need Jesus to rescue me from…

- *Discuss*: During training or combat, how can Jesus rescue me?

God, thank you for always following through on your promised rescue! Amen.

Weekly Memory Verse

All this took place to fulfill what the Lord had spoken by the prophet: "Behold, the virgin shall conceive and bear a son, and they shall call his name Immanuel" (which means, God with us). (Matthew 1:22-23)

Jesus, Point Man (Day 2)

Jesus, Our Servant Leader – Mark

> And he said to them, "Do not be alarmed. You seek Jesus of Nazareth, who was crucified. He has risen; he is not here. See the place where they laid him." (Mark 16:6)

Reflect

As we know in the military, actions speak louder than words.

The Gospel of Mark is an action-packed story about the life of Christ. Mark focuses less on what Jesus says and more on what Jesus does, through eighteen miracles. Rather than describing him as an action hero, Mark casts the Son of God as a suffering servant. The beauty of God's methods is how different they are from ours. Jesus is the hero who came to rescue us, but he doesn't swoop in with fanfare and a protocol team.

Instead, **Mark portrays Jesus as God, but a God who stooped down to serve**. Jesus came to earth to die, which is why much of the book details Jesus's journey to the cross. Some have described Mark as a passion (or suffering) story with an introduction. No doubt the focus rests on Jesus's sacrificial death—a sacrifice born out of love, and a desire to save and protect.

This is the climax of the story. This is all that really matters.

As military women, we are quite familiar with the ideas of service and sacrifice. So, when we serve our country, our family, and our neighbors, we reflect the love, service, and sacrifice that Jesus modeled.

On Point: The Gospel of Mark shows us Jesus is the ultimate servant leader.

- *Journal*: Sacrifice and service are hallmarks of strong leadership because...

- *Journal*: When I think about Jesus's sacrifice, I am inspired to...

- *Discuss*: How can we prevent resentment from building up when we serve others?

Jesus, thank you for modeling what authentic service and sacrifice looks like. Amen.

All this took place to fulfill what the Lord had spoken by the prophet: "Behold, the virgin shall conceive and bear a son, and they shall call his name Immanuel" (which means, God with us.) (Matthew 1:22-23)

Jesus, Point Man (Day 3)

Jesus Came for All – Luke

Read

> It seemed good to me also, having followed all things
> closely for some time past, to write an orderly account
> for you, most excellent Theophilus, that you may have
> certainty concerning the things you have been taught.
> (Luke 1:3-4)

Reflect

We live in an age of virtual reality. How can you be certain
something is true? Facts, details, eyewitness accounts, and
evidence are some of the things that take us from gray to
black-and-white. Luke was a physician, so facts, details, and
first-person testimonies were essential to his storytelling. Luke
wanted certainty.

As a doctor, Luke highlighted Jesus as a compassionate healer.
Luke's account of Jesus's life includes more healing stories
than any of the other Gospels. Like Luke, we are in front-line
professions as military women who deal with real-world issues
and difficulties.

Luke was also the only Gentile (non-Jewish) writer of the Bible.
As such, he wove in more explanations and descriptions of
Jewish customs and traditions so that non-Jewish people may
better understand the life of Christ. The most distinguishing
characteristic of this Gospel, however, is Luke showing that
Jesus came for all people—not just Jews, not just men.

The gospel is universal.

Luke shows us a Savior who engaged with men, women, children, outcasts, the poor, the sick, and the sinners. No one is outside Jesus's reach, Jesus's love, Jesus's healing touch. Of this, we can be certain.

On Point: The Gospel of Luke reminds us that the good news of God is for everyone.

Respond

- *Journal*: Knowing the details of Jesus's life helps me understand…
- *Journal*: If Jesus came for all people, then…
- *Discuss*: How might Jesus help me deal with my military challenges?

Jesus, thank you for loving us no matter who we are. Amen.

Weekly Memory Verse

All this took place to fulfill what the Lord had spoken by the prophet: "Behold, the virgin shall conceive and bear a son, and they shall call his name Immanuel" (which means, God with us.) (Matthew 1:22-23)

Jesus, Point Man (Day 4)

Jesus is God – John

> Now Jesus did many other signs in the presence of the disciples, which are not written in this book; but these are written so that you may believe that Jesus is the Christ, the Son of God, and that by believing you may have life in his name. (John 20:30-31)

Reflect

When we first start reading the Gospel of John, it's definitely not like the other three Gospels, even though some content is similar. If given a parachute or a life jacket from a different military branch, we can still believe that it will work properly.

John *believed* Jesus was God. He saw Jesus up close and personal. He was part of "the inner circle." So, when he wrote his Gospel, he provided proof after proof of Jesus's true identity:

- Changed lives (John the Baptist, Andrew, Peter, Nicodemus, the Samaritan woman)

- Miraculous signs (water into wine, feeding the 5,000, walking on water, raising Lazarus)

- Emphatic "I AM" statements (bread of life, light of the world, resurrection and the life)

While he wrote in simple terms about the life of Christ, John carefully conveyed deep spiritual truths along the way. John's "spiritual gospel" provided evidence that Jesus is God, and gave assurance that belief in Jesus leads to eternal life.

No, John did not include every detail of Jesus's life. You won't even find the story of Jesus's birth or home of record. What John does include, however, is everything we need to know to believe that Jesus is who he said he was. **It's hard to argue about changed lives**.

 The stresses of the military bump up against my trust in God. But when I look back on his faithfulness or forward to his promises, I experience renewed hope.

On Point: John repeatedly reminds us that believing in Jesus results in eternal life.

Respond

- *Journal*: I understand that belief in Jesus brings...
- *Journal*: Jesus has changed my life by...
- *Discuss*: How does believing in Jesus impact your military assignment?

God, thank you for sending Jesus so that I may live forever with you. Amen.

Weekly Memory Verse

All this took place to fulfill what the Lord had spoken by the prophet: "Behold, the virgin shall conceive and bear a son, and they shall call his name Immanuel" (which means, God with us.) (Matthew 1:22-23)

Jesus, Point Man (Day 5)
Powered by the Holy Spirit – Acts

Read

> "But you will receive power when the Holy Spirit has come upon you, and you will be my witnesses in Jerusalem, and in all Judea and Samaria, and to the end of the earth." (Acts 1:8)

Reflect

Do you enjoy sequels? If so, you might enjoy Acts, which tells what happened after Jesus went up into heaven. Luke, the doctor-turned-author, follows characters previously introduced in his first volume (like Peter) and introduces new characters (like Paul) who help to advance the message about Jesus well beyond Jerusalem.

Perhaps the most important character of the sequel, however, is the Holy Spirit (aka the Helper). The Holy Spirit's appearance in the book of Acts shows the power God infuses into believers. Throughout the Scriptures, the commander's presence on the battlefield is essential and effective. The Holy Spirit goes with us into the battles as well as the basic moments of life. After Jesus ascended into heaven, the Holy Spirit came. God with us. Read about it in Acts!

The boldness, certainty, and energy the Holy Spirit gives enables the messengers of Jesus to turn the world upside down (Acts 17:6). By the end of Acts, the truth about Jesus has been projected to Rome, and thousands have believed in the only name under heaven by which humankind can be saved (Acts 4:12). Consider reading Acts in one sitting—or Luke and Acts together—and see for yourself the evidence of the Holy Spirit's power in people, as described in Acts:

- – 3,000 converts in one day (Acts 2:41)
- – Signs and wonders (Acts 5:12)
- – Boldness and perseverance despite persecution (Acts 5:41-42)
- – Conversion of a rabid persecutor (Acts 9)

On Point: The Holy Spirit empowers ordinary men and women to change the world.

Respond

- – *Journal*: I understand that the Holy Spirit is...
- – *Journal*: I can rely on the Holy Spirit for...
- – *Discuss*: How can we fully experience the Holy Spirit on the battlefield?

God, make me a vessel the Holy Spirit can empower! Amen.

Weekly Memory Verse

All this took place to fulfill what the Lord had spoken by the prophet: "Behold, the virgin shall conceive and bear a son, and they shall call his name Immanuel" (which means, God with us.) (Matthew 1:22-23)

Letters to Churches (Day 1)

SOP of Salvation – Romans

Read

> There is therefore now no condemnation for those who are in Christ Jesus. (Romans 8:1)

Reflect

Every unit budget requires us to follow standard operating procedures. Sometimes we find ourselves in debt—a larger debt than we can pay. Likewise, but on a much more significant scale, sin is a debt we were—and are—unable to pay. Paul, the author of Romans, reminds us that God sent his Son Jesus to pay our debt in full.

Paul writes to the people of Rome, a people he has not yet visited. Paul writes to encourage them to trust Christ for salvation and then live that out, starting by trading in sin. According to Romans 8:1, whereas sin would condemn us, Christ saves us. This is very good news!

Romans reinforces our inability to change by simply "being a good person." **We need to be "God people"—not just good people—covered by, and deeply dependent upon, the blood of Christ**. Only Christ can save us through our faith in him. Salvation means a new life in Christ for every believer. Romans is like the SOP of salvation in Christ—the what, why, and how.

Although I have put my faith in Jesus Christ, I sometimes sin or miss God's mark. When I do, the debt feels even greater, somehow. I take confidence in Romans 8:1 that Christ always forgives and removes my condemnation. I desire to remain "in Christ" from here on out.

On Point: The blood of Jesus declares the Christian "not guilty" before a holy God.

Respond

- *Journal*: When I think of my debt of sin and the price Christ paid, I...
- *Journal*: When I am walking by faith, I feel...
- *Discuss*: How can I apply the SOP of salvation to the same degree that I apply military regulations?

Lord, thank you for letters of assurance and instruction, like Romans. Amen.

Weekly Memory Verse

There is therefore now no condemnation for those who are in Christ Jesus. (Romans 8:1)

Letters to Churches (Day 2)

Attention to Orders! – 1 & 2 Corinthians

Read

> For I decided to know nothing among you except Jesus Christ and him crucified. (1 Corinthians 2:2)

Reflect

"Attention to orders!" This means "pay attention" for military personnel, right? Stop what you are doing and focus on the upcoming commands. Paul, the author of 1 and 2 Corinthians, is giving his full attention, focus, purpose, and energy to knowing who Jesus is and what Jesus has done. And he tells the church at Corinth to do the same.

As followers of Christ, we must also pay attention. We have a new identity, a new commander, and new marching orders. We are new creations, born from above and changed from within.

Christians face tests of faith, but in these struggles we are to commit to follow Christ. As military women, the ways we do our jobs depend on our branch, unit, and mission. As Christians, we have a common mission to know Christ and him crucified. And to live like we know Christ!

Paul's letters instruct the Corinthians to be unified in their mission, stressing the need to deal with sinfulness within the church. He entreated the Corinthians to reject teachings that caused them to stumble and embrace Paul's suffering as a mark of his submission to Christ. We, too, may stumble and fall into deception in our Christian walk. **But as believers, we can overcome deception by prayer and the study of God's Word**.

Through the Scriptures, we can identify and correct sinful behavior. We must keep at it!

 Suzanne deals with chronic pain, which can go two ways spiritually. Either she stands by God for comfort and healing, or she distances herself from God. She makes a daily decision to pay "attention to orders" and draws near to Christ by praising God in word and song.

On Point: Attention to orders! Paul's letters call us to focus on Christ.

Respond

- *Journal*: Paul's letters call us to focus on Christ because…

- *Journal*: In what ways do I need to pay more "attention to orders" spiritually?

- *Discuss*: Why does faith require vigilance?

Lord, thank you for Christ's death and resurrection. Help me keep my focus there! Amen.

Weekly Memory Verse

There is therefore now no condemnation for those who are in Christ Jesus. (Romans 8:1)

Letters to Churches (Day 3)

Armored Up! – Galatians and Ephesians

> For freedom Christ has set us free; stand firm therefore, and do not submit again to a yoke of slavery. (Galatians 5:1)

Reflect

When we train or deploy, we shape our efforts with a certain population or culture in mind. Paul does the same thing in writing his letters to the believers in Galatia and Ephesus—cities in the Roman Empire, now modern-day Turkey. They needed to know how to live as Christians.

The Galatians were facing a type of Stockholm syndrome, where victims bond with their captor and no longer desire freedom. The Galatian Christians were used to centuries of Old Testament law, in the same way oxen become used to the weight of the plow. Learning to live in Christ—without the heavy rituals and system of blood sacrifice—was a hard transition. Paul encouraged them to stand firm in the sufficiency of Christ's sacrifice and freedom. A survival strategy can be found in Galatians 5:22-23 outlining the "fruit of the Spirit."

Paul had lived among the Ephesians for two years, and was now writing to reinforce his teaching. Paul's instructions to the Ephesians are very practical and focus on how they should "walk in a manner worthy" of Christ (Ephesians 4:1). If you want a practical book on Christian living, read Ephesians. Key words and phrases include grace, peace, love, and being in Christ.

Galatians and Ephesians challenge us to stand firmly in the faith and freedom of Christ. To accomplish this, we rely on the guidance and power of the Holy Spirit.

On Point: Galatians and Ephesians persuade us to move out in Christ, by the power of the Spirit.

Respond

- *Journal*: The aspects of the fruit of the Spirit listed in Galatians 5:22-23 are...

- Journal: Freedom in Christ is...

- *Discuss*: What keeps us from moving out in Christ?

Lord, thank you for setting me free. Please help me walk in your freedom. Amen.

Weekly Memory Verse

There is therefore now no condemnation for those who are in Christ Jesus. (Romans 8:1)

Letters to Churches (Day 4)

Run the Race! – Philippians and Colossians

Read

> I press on toward the goal for the prize of the upward call of God in Christ Jesus. (Philippians 3:14)

Reflect

We are learning that the Word of God is powerful and very helpful to our routine lives. Does anyone in the military have a routine life?! **God's Word reaches in and helps out**!

Paul dealt with several themes in his letters to the Philippians and Colossians. These super helpful books draw a stark contrast between the world's way of doing things vs. God's ways, giving lots of practical guidelines to help master the basics.

Humility and self-sacrifice are not easy to achieve. One of the ironies of military life is its dual culture of service and competition. Paul offers practical encouragement about the prize on which to fix our eyes. While we might gain worldly rank or promotion in the process, our focus must be service to Christ.

Colossians reinforces this mindset by emphasizing Jesus's supremacy, our spiritual fullness, freedom from human rules, and plenty of helpful instructions.

I felt brokenhearted—and broken—when I wasn't selected for command. When had my hope switched from Christ to kudos? A godly friend wisely said, "It's hard not to get something the world calls a prize." Staying in God's Word helps keep my eyes on the right goal.

On Point: Philippians and Colossians remind us to keep our eyes on Christ in the race of life!

Respond

- *Journal*: The Christian life is like a race because...
- Journal: To better keep my eyes on Christ, I need to ask God...
- *Discuss*: How can a Christian manage service vs. competition in the military?

Lord, help me keep my eye on the prize of Jesus Christ. Amen.

Weekly Memory Verse

There is therefore now no condemnation for those who are in Christ Jesus. (Romans 8:1)

Letters to Churches (Day 5)

Firm Under Fire – 1 & 2 Thessalonians

Read

> Rejoice always, pray without ceasing, give thanks in all circumstances; for this is the will of God in Christ Jesus for you. (1 Thessalonians 5:16-18)

Reflect

Standing firm under fire. It's not easy! Have you ever been persecuted for your faith?

In 1 and 2 Thessalonians, Paul encourages a body of relatively new converts facing doubt and religious persecution. The citizens of Thessalonica, the second-largest city in Greece today, faced a toxic command climate. People were being stoned, beaten, tortured, and even crucified. Paul understood that being a follower of Christ meant you gave up everything to follow Christ. Like us, the Thessalonians needed hope.

Christ's endurance on the cross is a model of perseverance for all Christians. And our hope comes with the truth that Jesus, our redeemer, lives—and he lives in us—giving us courage to stand firm in the Lord. We can also look forward to our reward in heaven—a promise Paul reminds the Thessalonians to hold to while under fire.

Today, Christians around the world face persecution for following Christ. Let's pray for their strength, endurance, witness, and faithfulness. And let's pray for our own courage. Let's read Paul's prayer in 2 Thessalonians 3:5: *May the Lord direct your hearts to the love of God and to the steadfastness of Christ.* Amen! May it be so for us and fellow believers worldwide.

On Point: 1 and 2 Thessalonians remind us that the Lord gives us the strength to stand firm.

- *Journal*: In what ways have people been persecuted for their faith?
- Journal: How do I follow the instructions in 1 Thessalonians 5:16-18?
- *Discuss*: While in the military, how might I face religious persecution?

Lord, may you direct our hearts to the love of God and to the steadfastness of Christ. Amen.

There is therefore now no condemnation for those who are in Christ Jesus. (Romans 8:1)

Letters to Individuals and General Instructions (Day 1)

Mentors Matter – 1 & 2 Timothy, Titus, Philemon

Read

> I thank him who has given me strength, Christ Jesus our Lord, because he judged me faithful, appointing me to his service. (1 Timothy 1:12)

Reflect

Do you have a good mentor in the military? A watchful and perceptive advisor? That's Paul's role in his four letters to individuals—two letters to Timothy, one to Titus, and one to Philemon.

Paul's letters to individuals can speak to us individually about loving and leading well.

Paul is Titus's mentor as Titus came to faith through Paul's ministry (Titus 1:4). This letter gives instructions to Titus on setting up an orderly church. In Titus, Paul addresses the qualifications of leaders, and how they can train others to live and lead.

Philemon is a church leader and beloved brother in the faith. Paul comes alongside him to urge him on a delicate matter: his runaway slave, Onesimus, has met Paul and converted to Christianity. Paul urges Philemon to receive Onesimus as a brother, not a slave, upon his return.

Like Titus, Timothy is a young pastor and protégé of Paul. Paul sends his first letter to Timothy giving instructions on sound teaching and godly living. In his second letter, Paul is near death. He emphasizes once again for Timothy the importance of guarding and preaching the gospel and living it out.

At one assignment, I had a really hard time finding other Christians to connect with. I couldn't find a Bible study group and it was hard to commit to just one church. After "church shopping" for a while I quit trying. After that I stopped trying to please God. Thankfully God pursued, forgave, and restored me. Finding local fellowship is now a priority after a move.

On Point: Paul's letters to individuals can speak to us individually about loving and leading well.

Respond

- *Journal*: How can I serve the Lord through serving others?

- Journal: When I think of church attendance and participation, I…

- *Discuss*: In what ways does church attendance help the Christian grow strong?

God, please help me grow as part of your community of believers. Amen.

Weekly Memory Verse

Who is wise and understanding among you? By his good conduct let him show his works in the meekness of wisdom. (James 3:13)

Letters to Individuals and General Instructions (Day 2)

Jesus is Best – Hebrews

Read

> Long ago, at many times and in many ways, God spoke to our fathers by the prophets, but in these last days he has spoken to us by his Son, whom he appointed the heir of all things, through whom also he created the world. He is the radiance of the glory of God and the exact imprint of his nature, and he upholds the universe by the word of his power. (Hebrews 1:1-3a)

Reflect

I love coupons. A lot. I remember my first trip to the commissary. Coupons were everywhere! It was like Christmas came early. One year I got ground turkey nearly free with coupons. Our faith walk is similar in that nuggets of blessing and redemption are spread throughout the Bible.

Coupons of righteousness are everywhere in God's Word. Hebrews is full of promises of salvation and strength to keep going even in the face of adversity. Jesus is the face of a compassionate and understanding servant-leader who will fight for us. When we put our trust in Jesus, he will not disappoint those who love him. Hebrews tells us not that Jesus is good or better, but that Jesus is the best. To continue our commissary analogy, we can swing from joy over savings to frustration over checkout lines that wrap around several aisles. We need to fix our faith on eternal truth and not the circumstances of the moment. Such distractions can quickly lead to despair and defeat if we forget our true source of joy. Hebrews reminds us we are people of faith. Our Savior is able to redeem even our hardships. Remember this from Hebrews: 1) Jesus is best and 2) We are to walk "by faith."

On Point: Hebrews tells us not that Jesus is good or better, but that Jesus is the best.

Respond

- *Journal*: What makes Jesus the best, according to Hebrews 1:1-3a?

- *Journal*: If I am called to walk by faith, then...

- *Discuss*: Describe the best inspirational leader you've encountered. Take a few minutes and read Hebrews 11, the Hall of Faith. Which character stands out to you and why?

Lord, thank you for giving your Son, Jesus. He's the best! Please help me walk by faith. Amen.

Weekly Memory Verse

Who is wise and understanding among you? By his good conduct let him show his works in the meekness of wisdom. (James 3:13)

Letters to Individuals and General Instructions (Day 3)

Become Qualified – James and 1 & 2 Peter

Read

> Who is wise and understanding among you? By his good conduct let him show his works in the meekness of wisdom. (James 3:13)

Reflect

We all learn differently by listening, watching, and doing. While training others, someone might ask, "Show me again how that works?" The Word of God trains us and we grow in experience, mastery, and wisdom.

The books of James, 1 Peter, and 2 Peter are written to broad Christian audiences across the Roman Empire. They are among the most practical books in the Bible. James gives more than 60 instructions on how to live as Christians, walking in Christ's life-giving ways.

In 1 and 2 Peter, believers are told how to stand firm against suffering and religious persecution. One way is by remembering the glory to come. Peter writes from personal experience. Peter was with Jesus at his crucifixion, and Peter's own martyrdom was foretold by Christ (John 21:18-19).

James teaches how to live and love well and wisely. **Peter teaches that both external enemies (the world, the flesh and the devil) and internal enemies (lies we believe) are defeated by the standard of God's truth**. So, we practice our faith again and again and again.

On Point: James and Peter tell us how to live wisely and steadfastly for God.

- *Journal*: I need God's wisdom and perseverance to...
- *Journal*: I could use today's verse during the duty day by...
- *Discuss*: What external and internal enemies do we fight as a culture? As individuals?

Lord, thank you for showing me how to live out my faith and stand firm in Christ. Amen.

Who is wise and understanding among you? By his good conduct let him show his works in the meekness of wisdom. (James 3:13)

Letters to Individuals and General Instructions (Day 4)

Move Out! – 1, 2, & 3 John and Jude

Read

> Now to him who is able to keep you from stumbling and to present you blameless before the presence of his glory with great joy, to the only God, our Savior, through Jesus Christ our Lord, be glory, majesty, dominion, and authority, before all time and now and forever. Amen. (Jude 24-25)

Reflect

"Fall in!" is a command we quickly respond to in the military. When we hear a cadence being called, we know a unit might be on a formation run. Such sounds represent people working together. But what if only one person made it to formation? What if someone called cadence for themselves? Going solo minimizes our impact. The same applies spiritually.

There is a sense in which we "fall in" regarding faith—both individually and corporately. The books of 1, 2, & 3 John and Jude speak to right and wrong ways of living and loving. You can read these books—together—in about 20 minutes. And you should! Don't just get second-hand information about the Bible. Read it for yourself.

John of 1, 2, & 3 John is most likely the same person who wrote the Gospel of John and Revelation. He writes to encourage confidence in God and draw a contrast with false teaching. He wants his readers and hearers to truly understand the community connection between love, truth, and obedience.

Jude was Jesus's half-brother. In this short but very serious letter, Jude writes to warn against sin. Jude is uncompromisingly direct and honest about sin. We need to reject sinful behavior in our own lives and in our faith communities. The world is often untruthful and misleading. Look, really look, at those who stand in formation with you. Extend yourself beyond your comfort zone. Practice hospitality. Include others. Talk about truth and love. Build relationships within your military family. Then show them, through words and deeds, that all are welcome to join the greatest family of all, the family of God. Your marching orders are clear. Move out, and bring others with you!

On Point: The letters of John and Jude remind us to stand for and share God's love and truth.

Respond

- *Journal*: If you were asked about Jesus Christ, what would you say about him?

- *Journal*: Situations in which I've been confronted with immorality and falsehood are...

- *Discuss*: Ways I could get to know others in my unit include...

Lord, thank you for your love. Give us boldness to stand for your truth. Amen.

Weekly Memory Verse

Who is wise and understanding among you? By his good conduct let him show his works in the meekness of wisdom. (James 3:13)

Letters to Individuals and General Instructions (Day 5)

Best. Ending. Ever. – Revelation

Read

> Blessed is the one who reads aloud the words of this prophecy, and blessed are those who hear, and who keep what is written in it, for the time is near (Revelation 1:3).

Reflect

We come to the close of our journey through the New Testament. Like any assignment, we've dealt with the outrageous, impossible, and unbelievable. We've met heroes and villains, and we've met Jesus the Savior. The last book of the whole Bible, Revelation, is full of promises and blessings for Christians.

As women warriors, we train for our final assignment—a place the Lord is preparing for us. The sword of truth will defeat the lies of the enemy. More warriors like you will answer the call and will stand, together, victorious over evil. No more tears. No more sorrow.

Revelation tells us this life is a battle but Jesus wins. We are exhorted to stand watch for the return of the beloved commander, Jesus. We are reminded of the vital importance of staying alert and practicing spiritual readiness.

When my name is on the roll call of Jesus, I know that the Savior of the entire universe will be front and center. I will worship him face-to-face, forever!

Best. Ending. Ever.

On Point: This life is not the end. Revelation reminds us of an eternity with Jesus.

- *Journal*: If this life is not all there is…
- *Journal*: I can focus more on Jesus by…
- *Discuss*: The Bible says eternal life with Christ is real. What does this mean for life?

God, thank you for your victory and eternity in Christ for believers! Amen.

Who is wise and understanding among you? By his good conduct let him show his works in the meekness of wisdom. (James 3:13)

BIBLE BOOT CAMP FOR MILITARY WOMEN

Congratulations

You have completed Challenge 3! Psalm 119:130 says, "The unfolding of your words gives light." And we hope that's been your experience whether you tackled this Challenge as an individual or part of a small group.

Super Congratulations if you completed all three Challenges. If not, dig out that determination and read the other two Challlenges!

Appendixes

How to Read the Bible for Personal Study
Appendix A

> Let the word of Christ dwell in you richly, teaching and admonishing one another in all wisdom... (Colossians 3:16a)

Studying the Bible for personal use is life-changing! We are lifelong learners, and we are transformed by what we learn when we read God's Word. We can study the Bible in a group or alone in our quarters. We study the Bible to get answers, gain guidance, avoid wrong teaching, and to know God. Reading the Bible increases our spiritual awareness.

Our approach to the Bible matters:

- *Approach the Bible in prayer.* Ask the Holy Spirit to use God's Word to transform you.

- *Approach the Bible with expectancy.* Expect to encounter God in his living Word.

- *Approach the Bible carefully.* Read verses in context, asking who, what, and why.

- *Approach the Bible thoughtfully.* Consider using a paper and pen for reflection.

Where to Start

If you're not using a study guide like this one, starting with the New Testament can be helpful. Afterwards, read the Old Testament to get a bigger picture. Try reading Bible books from the beginning—even just a chapter at a time—for context. As you read, ask yourself: 1) What do I learn about God? and 2) How should I respond?

When to Read the Bible

You can read the Bible anytime! Many people like to read the Bible first thing in the morning to frame their day. You don't have to read the Bible just once a day. Anytime you have a few moments for reflection and meditation, the Bible is great inspiration—especially Psalms and Proverbs. Lighter duty days and weekends can be good times for extended study or longer readings.

Study Aids

Many good study Bibles have comments and explanations. Consider reading the Scripture before turning to the notes. A good study Bible gives some background on each book, and tells who wrote it, when and why. If you have questions or concerns, find a solid Bible teacher, chaplain or Christian friend to help you. The Lord has provided gifted teachers who correctly understand and obey the truth. A good teacher, like a good drill sergeant, helps us learn the right way to keep in step.

Bottom Line

Approach the Bible prayerfully and humbly for a deeper understanding. Study the verses in context and seek explanations from mature, seasoned Christians.

How to Memorize Scripture
Appendix B

> I have stored up your word in my heart…
> (Psalm 119:11a)

Storing God's Word in our heart means we have the truth whenever and wherever we need it. We do this by memorizing key verses. Memorization allows Scripture to "take root."

Our generation has more information at our fingertips than ever. Our smartphones, iPads and personal computers are readily available. Technically, we don't have to memorize anything. Even the latest SOP (Standard Operating Procedure) for the unit is available at our fingertips.

Still, memorizing information—especially the Holy Scriptures—is essential. Smartphones break, iPads lose energy, and we can't carry our computer all the time. We must remember important information. A pilot can't always fly on autopilot. I understand it's not easy. Our memory muscles need development. The more we use our memory muscle, the stronger it gets.

Tips for Memorizing Scripture

- Find a quiet place, free from distractions
- Read the verse(s) at least three times: first for the eyes, second for the mind, third for the heart
- Say the verse out loud—speak it with understanding
- Write it down. Carry it with you and refer to it during down times (in line, etc.)

- Read the passage at night before lights out. You will be amazed what your mind does while you are sleeping! You may awake with the words on your tongue!

As we know in the military, memorization can be a little frustrating at first. But the rewards are remarkable. Take your time. Remember how hard it was to memorize everyone's rank? Now you can recall ranks without a second thought.

Memorizing helps us capture each word and remember it in the future. Being involved with the verse makes memorization easier. Other methods of memorization, such as using music, might help you. Try posting sticky notes in your cover or on the edge of a mirror. Use hand signals or, if you're able, translate the verse into a different language. Repetition is important.

The goal is to let God's Word get deep into the recesses of your heart. Having a memorized verse spring up at just the right moment is encouraging and life-changing!

How to Pray

Appendix C

> And he [Jesus] told them a parable to the effect that they ought always to pray and not lose heart. (Luke 18:1)

When we pray, we reach out to God. In the reaching, our attitude and spiritual awareness are revolutionized. Prayer is not some magical formula to get the right results. God is not a magician. Prayer invites us into relationship. God desires real and personal communication with us. He's more interested in what concerns us than how we pray. Prayer is personal.

In Matthew 6:9-13—called the Lord's Prayer—Jesus taught his disciples to pray. Many people use this as a pattern for prayer, and others use it as a daily prayer. Some even do both!

> Pray then like this: "Our Father in heaven, hallowed be your name. Your kingdom come, your will be done, on earth as it is in heaven. Give us this day our daily bread, and forgive us our debts, as we also have forgiven our debtors. And lead us not into temptation, but deliver us from evil." (Matthew 6:9-13)

The book of Psalms is full of beautiful prayers. We can echo these prayers to God, or we can speak to him and praise him freely and personally. Though we can (and should) pray anywhere, Jesus often took extended periods of time and went to solitary places to pray. What should we pray about? Philippians gives us some clues:

The Lord is at hand; do not be anxious about anything, but in everything by prayer and supplication with thanksgiving let your requests be made known to God. And the peace of God which surpasses all understanding, will guard your hearts and your minds in Christ Jesus. (Philippians 4:5b-7)

When you pray, remember this:

- *"Draw near to God, and he will draw near to you"* (James 4:8a). Prayer is personal!

- *Pray about everything.* There are no secrets with the all-knowing God.

- *Pray with confidence.* God is not judging the delivery of your prayers!

- *Pray with thankfulness.* Gratitude is one of God's means to guard our hearts.

"Thus says the LORD who made the earth, the LORD who formed it to establish it—the LORD is his name: Call to me and I will answer you, and will tell you great and hidden things that you have not known." (Jeremiah 33:2-3)

Being a Christian
Appendix D

> "Sirs, what must I do to be saved?" And they [Paul & Silas] said, "Believe in the Lord Jesus, and you will be saved..." And he rejoiced along with his entire household that he had believed in God. (Acts 16: 30-31b, 34b)

What does it mean to be a Christian? It means believing in the Lord Jesus for salvation.

A Christian is a Christ-follower or a disciple of Christ. Being a Christian is much like being a military service member—it takes the commitment of whole-hearted faith and trust. Being a Christian means bearing Christ's name and surrendering to his leadership—sometimes at great personal cost. Our choice to become a service member is only for a short time, but our commitment to Christ lasts a lifetime—and beyond.

Christianity is more than a religion. It's a relationship with Christ.

If the idea of being a Christian is new to you, consider the following truths from the Bible:

- *John 14:6* – Jesus said to him, "I am the way, and the truth, and the life. No one comes to the Father except through me."

- *John 3:16* – "For God so loved the world, that he gave his only Son, that whoever believes in him should not perish but have eternal life."

- *1 Peter 3:18* – For Christ also suffered once for sins, the righteous for the unrighteous, that he might bring us to God, being put to death in the flesh but made alive in the spirit.

– *1 John 1:9* – If we confess our sins, he is faithful and just to forgive us our sins and to cleanse us from all unrighteousness.

It simply takes a prayer...

Lord Jesus, I know I have sinned against you. I come to you today with a repentant heart asking you to forgive my sin. I believe you are the Son of God. You came to earth and chose to die on the cross for me, and then rose again so that I could have eternal life. Beginning today, I surrender my life to you. In the holy name of Jesus, I pray. Amen.

Facilitator's Guide

Appendix E

> But he [Jesus] answered, "It is written,
> 'Man shall not live by bread alone,
>   but by every word that comes from the mouth
>   of God.'" (Matthew 4:4)

How to Use this Bible Study

These three-week studies can be used individually or as a group. Each week includes:

- Five lessons
- Journal prompts for personal reflection
- Discussion prompts for group facilitation
- Memory verse

For Individual Use

- Read the whole lesson (should take about 5 minutes).
- Reflect on the journal prompts by writing your answers or thinking them through.
- Recite the weekly memory verse. You'll be surprised how it begins to stick and speak!

For Group Use

- Ideally, each participant would read the daily lessons.
- At the end of each week, gather to discuss that week's lessons. Focus on God!
- Begin your gathering with prayer, asking God to guide the discussion in truth.

- Use your time together to go over discussion (and perhaps journal) questions.

- End your time by looking at the weekly memory verse. What does it reveal about God?

- First, **introduce the big idea**—the chapter theme—such as "What is the Bible?"

- Second, **work through the Bible verses and discussion prompts**. These are found at the end of each lesson. Feel free to incorporate the journal questions into your discussion. This would give you 15 questions to choose from. *You know your group, so feel free to pick the questions that would be most relevant.*

- Third, **consider how the weekly memory verse supports the big idea**. Encourage participants to memorize the Scriptures. Model this by doing memory work yourself.

- Fourth, **share prayer requests, if appropriate** to your group dynamics.

- Finally, **pray for your participants** during the week. Encourage them in faith!

Daily Bible Reading Guide

This Daily Bible Reading Guide is based on the liturgical calendar year 2019. Feel free to read through these daily readings or go to DailyBible.AmericanBible.org and download and print a Daily Bible Reading Guide based on the current year. This site also allows you to enhance your daily Bible reading with a daily devotional keyed to the current year's daily reading.

As you read the Bible each day, allow the Scriptures to speak to you. This daily "dialogue" between you and the biblical text will reveal new understandings about God, and about yourself.

- **Pray** with focus and openness to see what God has for you. God connect me here, as I seek you in your Word.

- **Read** the selected passage of Scripture slowly. Take note of intriguing words and phrases. Read them a second time.

- **Reflect** on what strikes you as you read. Think through what God is communicating to you at this point in your life.

- **Respond** to the passage. Speak to God directly about what's on your mind and heart. Look for ways to live out what you've uncovered.

January

- [ ] 1   Hebrews 1:1-14
- [ ] 2   Hebrews 2:1-18
- [ ] 3   Hebrews 3:1-19
- [ ] 4   Luke 3:1-20
- [ ] 5   Luke 3:21-38
- [ ] 6   Matthew 2:1-12
- [ ] 7   Matthew 2:13-23
- [ ] 8   Luke 4:1-15
- [ ] 9   Luke 4:16-30
- [ ] 10   Luke 4:31-44
- [ ] 11   Luke 5:1-16
- [ ] 12   Luke 5:17-32
- [ ] 13   Luke 5:33—6:11
- [ ] 14   Luke 6:12-26
- [ ] 15   Luke 6:27-49
- [ ] 16   Luke 7:1-17
- [ ] 17   Luke 7:18-35
- [ ] 18   Luke 7:36—8:3
- [ ] 19   Luke 8:22-39
- [ ] 20   Luke 8:40-56
- [ ] 21   Luke 9:1-17
- [ ] 22   Luke 9:18-27
- [ ] 23   Luke 9:28-45
- [ ] 24   Luke 9:46-62
- [ ] 25   Luke 10:1-24
- [ ] 26   Luke 19:1-10
- [ ] 27   Colossians 1:1-23
- [ ] 28   Colossians 1:24—2:5
- [ ] 29   Colossians 2:6-19
- [ ] 30   Colossians 2:20—3:17
- [ ] 31   Colossians 4:2-18

February

- [ ] 1   Leviticus 19:1-18
- [ ] 2   Luke 10:25-37
- [ ] 3   John 1:19-34
- [ ] 4   John 1:35-51
- [ ] 5   John 2:1-12
- [ ] 6   John 2:13-25
- [ ] 7   John 3:1-21
- [ ] 8   John 3:22-36
- [ ] 9   John 5:1-18
- [ ] 10   John 5:19-47
- [ ] 11   John 6:1-21
- [ ] 12   John 6:22-40
- [ ] 13   John 6:41-71
- [ ] 14   John 7:1-24
- [ ] 15   John 7:25-52
- [ ] 16   John 8:1-20
- [ ] 17   John 8:21-47
- [ ] 18   John 8:48-59
- [ ] 19   John 10:1-21
- [ ] 20   John 10:22-42
- [ ] 21   1 John 1:1-10
- [ ] 22   1 John 2:1-17
- [ ] 23   1 John 2:18-29
- [ ] 24   1 John 3:1-24
- [ ] 25   1 John 4:1-21
- [ ] 26   1 John 5:1-21
- [ ] 27   2 John
- [ ] 28   3 John

March

- [ ] 1   Psalm 85
- [ ] 2   Psalm 89:1-18
- [ ] 3   Psalm 27
- [ ] 4   Psalm 30
- [ ] 5   Psalm 31
- [ ] 6   Psalm 32
- [ ] 7   Psalm 35
- [ ] 8   Psalm 38
- [ ] 9   Psalm 39
- [ ] 10   Psalm 41
- [ ] 11   Psalm 42
- [ ] 12   Psalm 43
- [ ] 13   Psalm 44
- [ ] 14   Psalm 55
- [ ] 15   Psalm 56
- [ ] 16   Psalm 57
- [ ] 17   Psalm 61
- [ ] 18   Psalm 62
- [ ] 19   Psalm 63
- [ ] 20   Psalm 64
- [ ] 21   1 Kings 3:1-15
- [ ] 22   1 Kings 8:1-21
- [ ] 23   1 Kings 8:22-40
- [ ] 24   1 Kings 8:41-53
- [ ] 25   1 Kings 8:54-66
- [ ] 26   Job 23:1-17
- [ ] 27   Job 27:1-11
- [ ] 28   Job 40:1-24
- [ ] 29   Job 41:1-34
- [ ] 30   Job 42:1-17
- [ ] 31   Jeremiah 42:1-22

April

- [ ] 1   John 11:1-27
- [ ] 2   John 11:28-57
- [ ] 3   Luke 14:1-14
- [ ] 4   Luke 14:15-35
- [ ] 5   Luke 15:1-10
- [ ] 6   Luke 15:11-32
- [ ] 7   Luke 16:1-18
- [ ] 8   Luke 16:19-31
- [ ] 9   Luke 17:1-19
- [ ] 10   Luke 17:20-37
- [ ] 11   Luke 18:1-17
- [ ] 12   Luke 18:18-43
- [ ] 13   Luke 19:11-27
- [ ] 14   Luke 19:28-48
- [ ] 15   Luke 20:1-18
- [ ] 16   Luke 20:19-47
- [ ] 17   Luke 22:1-30
- [ ] 18   Luke 22:31-71

☐ 19 Luke 23:1-43
☐ 20 Luke 23:44-56
☐ 21 Luke 24:1-12
☐ 22 Luke 24:13-53
☐ 23 1 Peter 1:1-25
☐ 24 1 Peter 2:1-25
☐ 25 1 Peter 3:1-22
☐ 26 1 Peter 4:1-19
☐ 27 1 Peter 5:1-14
☐ 28 2 Peter 1:1-21
☐ 29 2 Peter 2:1-22
☐ 30 2 Peter 3:1-18

May

☐ 1 Joshua 22:1-9
☐ 2 Joshua 22:10-34
☐ 3 Joshua 23:1-16
☐ 4 Joshua 24:1-33
☐ 5 Judges 1:1-36
☐ 6 Judges 2:1-10
☐ 7 Judges 2:11-23
☐ 8 Judges 3:1-11
☐ 9 Judges 3:12-31
☐ 10 Judges 4:1-24
☐ 11 Judges 5:1-31
☐ 12 Judges 6:1-27
☐ 13 Judges 6:28-40
☐ 14 Judges 7:1-25
☐ 15 Judges 8:1-35
☐ 16 Judges 9:1-21
☐ 17 Judges 9:22-57
☐ 18 Judges 10:1-18
☐ 19 Judges 11:1-28
☐ 20 Judges 11:29-40
☐ 21 Judges 12:1-15
☐ 22 Judges 13:1-25
☐ 23 Judges 14:1-20
☐ 24 Judges 15:1-20
☐ 25 Judges 16:1-31
☐ 26 Ruth 1:1-22
☐ 27 Ruth 2:1-23
☐ 28 Ruth 3:1-18
☐ 29 Ruth 4:1-22
☐ 30 Acts 1:1-11
☐ 31 Acts 1:12-26

June

☐ 1 Psalm 47
☐ 2 Galatians 1:1-24
☐ 3 Galatians 2:1-21
☐ 4 Galatians 3:1-14
☐ 5 Galatians 3:15—4:7
☐ 6 Galatians 4:8-31
☐ 7 Galatians 5:1-26
☐ 8 Galatians 6:1-18
☐ 9 Acts 2:1-28
☐ 10 Acts 2:29-47
☐ 11 Acts 10:1-33
☐ 12 Acts 10:34-48
☐ 13 Acts 11:1-18
☐ 14 Acts 11:19-30
☐ 15 Acts 12:1-25
☐ 16 Acts 13:1-12
☐ 17 Acts 13:13-41
☐ 18 Acts 13:42-52
☐ 19 Acts 14:1-28
☐ 20 Acts 15:1-21
☐ 21 Acts 15:22-41
☐ 22 Acts 16:1-15
☐ 23 Acts 16:16-40
☐ 24 Acts 17:1-15
☐ 25 Acts 17:16-34
☐ 26 Romans 8:1-17
☐ 27 Romans 8:18-39
☐ 28 Romans 12:1-21
☐ 29 John 15:1-17
☐ 30 John 15:18—16:15

July

☐ 1 1 Samuel 1:1-18
☐ 2 1 Samuel 1:19-28
☐ 3 1 Samuel 2:1-11
☐ 4 1 Samuel 2:12-26
☐ 5 1 Samuel 2:27-36
☐ 6 1 Samuel 3:1-21
☐ 7 1 Samuel 6:1-19
☐ 8 1 Samuel 6:20—7:17
☐ 9 1 Samuel 8:1-22
☐ 10 1 Samuel 9:1-27
☐ 11 1 Samuel 10:1-16
☐ 12 1 Samuel 10:17-27
☐ 13 1 Samuel 12:1-25
☐ 14 1 Samuel 15:1-35
☐ 15 1 Samuel 16:1-23
☐ 16 1 Samuel 25:1-22
☐ 17 1 Samuel 25:23-44
☐ 18 1 Samuel 31:1-13
☐ 19 2 Samuel 1:1-27
☐ 20 2 Samuel 2:1—3:1
☐ 21 2 Samuel 5:1-25
☐ 22 2 Samuel 6:1-23
☐ 23 2 Samuel 7:1-17
☐ 24 2 Samuel 7:18-29
☐ 25 Psalm 89:19-37
☐ 26 2 Samuel 22:1-25
☐ 27 2 Samuel 22:26-51
☐ 28 Genesis 6:1-22
☐ 29 Genesis 7:1-24
☐ 30 Genesis 8:1-22
☐ 31 Genesis 9:1-29

August

- [ ] 1 Exodus 3:1-22
- [ ] 2 Exodus 4:1-17
- [ ] 3 Exodus 4:18-31
- [ ] 4 Exodus 5:1—6:1
- [ ] 5 Exodus 6:2-27
- [ ] 6 Exodus 6:28—7:13
- [ ] 7 Exodus 7:14-25
- [ ] 8 Exodus 8:1-19
- [ ] 9 Exodus 8:20-32
- [ ] 10 Exodus 9:1-12
- [ ] 11 Exodus 9:13-35
- [ ] 12 Exodus 10:1-20
- [ ] 13 Exodus 10:21-29
- [ ] 14 Exodus 11:1-10
- [ ] 15 Exodus 12:1-28
- [ ] 16 Exodus 12:29-51
- [ ] 17 Exodus 13:1-22
- [ ] 18 Exodus 14:1-31
- [ ] 19 Exodus 15:1-27
- [ ] 20 Exodus 16:1-21
- [ ] 21 Exodus 16:22-36
- [ ] 22 Exodus 17:1-16
- [ ] 23 Exodus 33:1-11
- [ ] 24 Exodus 33:12-23
- [ ] 25 Leviticus 16:1-19
- [ ] 26 Leviticus 16:20-34
- [ ] 27 Numbers 14:1-25
- [ ] 28 2 Samuel 9:1-13
- [ ] 29 2 Samuel 11:1-27
- [ ] 30 2 Samuel 12:1-25
- [ ] 31 Psalm 51

September

- [ ] 1 Luke 8:4-21
- [ ] 2 Luke 11:1-13
- [ ] 3 Luke 11:14-23
- [ ] 4 Luke 11:24-36
- [ ] 5 Luke 11:37-54
- [ ] 6 Luke 12:1-21
- [ ] 7 Luke 12:22-40
- [ ] 8 Luke 12:41-59
- [ ] 9 Luke 13:1-17
- [ ] 10 Luke 13:18-35
- [ ] 11 Psalm 15
- [ ] 12 Psalm 37
- [ ] 13 1 Corinthians 1:1-17
- [ ] 14 1 Corinthians 1:18-31
- [ ] 15 1 Corinthians 2:1-16
- [ ] 16 James 1:1-27
- [ ] 17 James 2:1-26
- [ ] 18 James 3:1-18
- [ ] 19 James 4:1-17
- [ ] 20 James 5:1-20
- [ ] 21 Psalm 119:1-24
- [ ] 22 Psalm 119:25-48
- [ ] 23 Psalm 119:49-64
- [ ] 24 Psalm 119:65-80
- [ ] 25 Psalm 119:81-96
- [ ] 26 Psalm 119:97-112
- [ ] 27 Psalm 119:113-128
- [ ] 28 Psalm 119:129-144
- [ ] 29 Psalm 119:145-160
- [ ] 30 Psalm 119:161-176

October

- [ ] 1 Exodus 20:1-17
- [ ] 2 Leviticus 25:1-22
- [ ] 3 Leviticus 25:23-38
- [ ] 4 Leviticus 25:39-55
- [ ] 5 Leviticus 26:1-13
- [ ] 6 Leviticus 26:14-46
- [ ] 7 Leviticus 27:1-15
- [ ] 8 Leviticus 27:16-34
- [ ] 9 Numbers 28:1-15
- [ ] 10 Numbers 28:16-31
- [ ] 11 Numbers 29:1-11
- [ ] 12 Numbers 29:12-40
- [ ] 13 Deuteronomy 1:1-18
- [ ] 14 Deuteronomy 4:1-14
- [ ] 15 Deuteronomy 4:15-40
- [ ] 16 Deuteronomy 4:41-49
- [ ] 17 Deuteronomy 5:1-22
- [ ] 18 Deuteronomy 5:23-33
- [ ] 19 Deuteronomy 6:1-25
- [ ] 20 Deuteronomy 7:1-11
- [ ] 21 Deuteronomy 7:12-26
- [ ] 22 Deuteronomy 8:1-20
- [ ] 23 Deuteronomy 10:1-22
- [ ] 24 Deuteronomy 16:18—17:13
- [ ] 25 Micah 1:1-16
- [ ] 26 Micah 2:1-13
- [ ] 27 Micah 3:1-12
- [ ] 28 Micah 4:1—5:1
- [ ] 29 Micah 5:2-15
- [ ] 30 Micah 6:1-16
- [ ] 31 Micah 7:1-20

November

- [ ] 1   Genesis 1:1—2:4a
- [ ] 2   Psalm 104
- [ ] 3   Psalm 105
- [ ] 4   Psalm 106
- [ ] 5   Psalm 107
- [ ] 6   Psalm 111
- [ ] 7   Psalm 112
- [ ] 8   Psalm 113
- [ ] 9   Psalm 114
- [ ] 10   Psalm 115
- [ ] 11   Psalm 116
- [ ] 12   Psalm 118
- [ ] 13   Psalm 132
- [ ] 14   Psalm 135
- [ ] 15   Psalm 136
- [ ] 16   Psalm 138
- [ ] 17   Psalm 18:1-24
- [ ] 18   Psalm 18:25-50
- [ ] 19   Psalm 21
- [ ] 20   Psalm 50
- [ ] 21   1 Chronicles 16:1-7
- [ ] 22   1 Chronicles 16:8-36
- [ ] 23   1 Chronicles 16:37-43
- [ ] 24   Psalm 144
- [ ] 25   Psalm 145
- [ ] 26   Psalm 146
- [ ] 27   Psalm 147
- [ ] 28   Psalm 148
- [ ] 29   Psalm 149
- [ ] 30   Psalm 150

December

- [ ] 1   Matthew 24:1-28
- [ ] 2   Matthew 24:29-51
- [ ] 3   Matthew 25:1-30
- [ ] 4   Matthew 25:31-46
- [ ] 5   Psalm 24
- [ ] 6   Psalm 91
- [ ] 7   Psalm 92
- [ ] 8   Psalm 93
- [ ] 9   Psalm 94
- [ ] 10   Psalm 95
- [ ] 11   Psalm 96
- [ ] 12   Psalm 97
- [ ] 13   Psalm 98
- [ ] 14   Psalm 99
- [ ] 15   Isaiah 8:1-20
- [ ] 16   Isaiah 8:21—9:7
- [ ] 17   Isaiah 60:1-22
- [ ] 18   Isaiah 61:1-11
- [ ] 19   Isaiah 62:1-12
- [ ] 20   Isaiah 63:1-14
- [ ] 21   Luke 1:1-25
- [ ] 22   Luke 1:26-56
- [ ] 23   Luke 1:57-80
- [ ] 24   Luke 2:1-21
- [ ] 25   John 1:1-18
- [ ] 26   Luke 2:22-52
- [ ] 27   Titus 1:1-16
- [ ] 28   Titus 2:1-15
- [ ] 29   Titus 3:1-15
- [ ] 30   Revelation 21:1-27
- [ ] 31   Revelation 22:1-21

Congratulations on completing the Daily Bible Reading Guide! Please take 5 minutes to tell us more about your experience and how this study impacted your life at: **ASMFeedback.com**

If you enjoyed this Daily Bible Reading Guide, go to **DailyBible.AmericanBible.org** and download Scripture readings for another year.

Contributors

 Claudia Duff serves as the assistant events coordinator and manager of the writing team for Planting Roots. She is a retired Navy wife and a past president and vice president of PWOC local, regional and International.

 Salena Duffy is an Army Veteran and she serves as a women's ministry leader and mentor in various capacities. She actively serves as Fort Carson Protestant Women of the Chapel (PWOC) Prayer Coordinator. She has served as the prayer coordinator at Planting Roots Ministry, as well as the military family liaison for Moms in Prayer International. In addition, she is a Bible study teacher, Precept Upon Precept instructor and public speaker.

 Kristin Goodrich is a Navy Veteran who is currently the executive officer at Planting Roots. She blogs on occasion, most recently about being a beginner ballet dancer.

 Muriel Gregory is a writer on the Planting Roots team and disciple-maker in the greater Kansas City area. Muriel is an Army wife and a Navy mom.

 Ginger Harrington is the publishing coordinator for Planting Roots and the author of *Holy in the Moment: Simple Ways to Love God and Enjoy Your Life*. An award-winning blogger and engaging speaker for military and civilian audiences, Ginger writes at GingerHarrington.com and PlantingRoots.net. A contributor for Heart Renovation and Breaking the Chains, Ginger has also edited and compiled *Free to Be Brave: Moments with God for Military Life.* Ginger and her retired Marine husband have been married for 28 years and have three young adult children. Visit Ginger's website or connect with her on Instagram @ GingerHarrington.

 Melissa Hicks serves as an editor and administrative assistant for Bible studies for Planting Roots. She is an Army BRAT and current Army wife.

 As a retired Army Officer, Suzanne Isaac is particularly passionate about serving and building up military women and spouses. Currently stationed at Fort Leavenworth, Kansas and married to a retired Army Officer, she is actively involved in various Chapel ministries and faithfully brings her passion for worship (with multiple instruments and harmony vocals) to the throne. She is also a worship team vocalist and instrumentalist for Planting Roots.

 Major (Retired) Christine Malkemes is a Vietnam era Veteran (Women's Army Corps), a military wife and a minister. As a humble member of the Christian faith, Reverend Malkemes is a Bible coach and mentor at Living Water Fellowship in Poinciana, Florida. She is a wife, mom, and writer. Her inspirational articles can be found at https://www.christinemalkemes.com

 Andrea Plotner serves as the Bible study coordinator for Planting Roots. A retired Army spouse and past-president of PWOC International, Andrea is the author of Beyond Brave and Outrageous Olives (https://thehubpwoc.net/outrageous-olives-2/).

Jennifer Wake is proudly married to an Army chaplain. She is a teacher, trainer and speaker. She has served on regional and local boards of PWOC wherever she has lived. She is the admin team lead for Planting Roots.

 Kori Yates serves as the director of Planting Roots. A former Marine and current Army wife, Kori is an author (Olive Drab Pom-Poms) and speaker. You can learn more at koriyates.com.